SPANISH TRAILS
A guide to walking in the Spanish mountains

THE SIERRA ALMIJARA AND TEJEDA
Hill Walks near Competa

BOOK TWO OF A SERIES

PHIL LAWLER

First Edition published 2018 by
Spanish Trails,
Skipton
North Yorkshire

Copyright © Phil Lawler
The right of Phil Lawler to be identified as the author
of this work has been asserted by him in accordance with the
Copyright, Designs and Patents Act 1988

All rights reserved. This book is sold subject to the condition that no part of this book is to be reproduced, in any shape or form. Or by way of trade, stored in a retrieval system or transmitted in any form or by any means, electronic, mechanical, photocopying, recording, be lent, re-sold, hired out or otherwise circulated in any form of binding or cover other than that in which it is published and without a similar condition, including this condition being imposed on the subsequent purchaser, without prior permission of the copyright holder.

Disclaimer

The author has taken all reasonable effort to ensure that the information herein is accurate, however the author accepts no responsibility if it is not, nor if unforeseen circumstances occur while doing the routes. We would also advise that in planning your route you check local transport, accommodation and please be aware that some paths and rights of way may be affected by changes such as development or weather. We would appreciate any information regarding changes. You can do this by contacting the Publisher in the first instance.

Photographs and Maps © 2018 Phil Lawler

The author has his own website: http://www.spanishtrailsco.com

Production by 2QT Limited (Publishing), Settle, North Yorkshire
Cover design by Charlotte Mouncey (using authors photograph)

Printed in Great Britain by
TJ Books Limited

A CIP catalogue record for this book is available
from the British Library
ISBN - 978-0-9955797-3-6

The author on La Maroma - **WALK 3**

DISCLAIMER

The walk descriptions and maps in this publication are as accurate as I can make them, but things change and I cannot guarantee that everything is always up to date or 100 per cent correct. You must take all reasonable precautions and wear adequate clothing, carry waterproofs, a mobile phone and so on, just as you would when hill walking in the UK. You also need protection from the sun. And let somebody know where you are going when you set out.

All users of this information do so entirely at their own risk.

ABOUT THE AUTHOR

I am a hill walker from Yorkshire. My job took me to live in Madrid, and I have worked in most big Spanish cities. I also lived in a hill village in Andalucia. I speak fluent Spanish, and I know the country well, with its varied landscapes, cultures and cuisine. I spent several years organising and guiding group walking tours in different parts of the country. .

In the Sierra Almijara and the Sierra Tejeda nowadays there is a network of great footpaths. With friends back in the nineties I physically cleared some of the old mule trails through the mountains. Many had been overgrown since the Spanish Civil War. There were no maps of these routes, and although mapping has improved many of the paths are still not shown. In those early days we never met another walker, but it has become a more popular walking area, with spectacular routes in a benign climate.

In recent years I have walked in several countries but so far I have seen nothing to beat the fantastic Spanish mountains.

CONTENTS

DISCLAIMER ... 3

ABOUT THE AUTHOR ... 4

ACKNOWLEDGEMENTS ... 9

ABOUT SPANISH TRAILS ... 10

THE SIERRA ALMIJARA AND TEJEDA ... 11

MAIN PEAKS OF THE SIERRA ALMIJARA AND TEJEDA ... 17

THE WALKS IN ORDER OF DIFFICULTY ... 18

SKETCH MAP OF WALK LOCATIONS ... 20

WALKS IN THE AXARQUIA ... 23

WALK NO. 1
ASCENT OF LA MAROMA FROM CANILLAS DE ACEITUNO ... 29

WALK NO. 2
LA MAROMA FROM LOS LLANOS DE SEDELLA ... 34

WALK NO. 3
LA MAROMA – CIRCUIT FROM CANILLAS DE ACEITUNO ... 39

WALK NO. 4
PUENTE COLGANTE/HANGING BRIDGE ... 45

WALK NO. 5
SEDELLA TO CANILLAS DE ACEITUNO ... 49

WALK NO. 6
SEDELLA TO THE SUMMIT OF EL FUERTE ... 53

WALK NO. 7
SEDELLA TO LOS PICARICOS ... 57

WALK NO. 8
CANILLAS DE ALBAIDA TO SEDELLA ... 62

WALK NO. 9
CANILLAS DE ALBAIDA TO SALARES ... 67

WALK NO. 10
CANILLAS DE ALBAIDA TO THE SUMMIT OF CERRO GAVILÁN, VIA CRUZ DE CANILLAS ... 73

WALK NO. 11
CASA DE LA MINA CIRCUIT ... 78

WALK NO. 12
CÓMPETA AND THE THREE VILLAGES WALK ... 83

WALK NO. 13
LA FÁBRICA DE LA LUZ TO CERRO VERDE AND CERRO ATALAYA ... 88

WALK NO. 14
MALAS CAMAS (1,792 METRES) FROM LA FÁBRICA ... 94

WALK NO. 15
EL LUCERO (1,764 METRES) FROM LA FÁBRICA DE LA LUZ ... 101

WALK NO. 16
EL LUCERO – CIRCUIT FROM PUERTO BLANQUILLO ... 106

WALK NO. 17
THE SILK ROUTE AND LA FÁBRICA ... 110

WALK NO. 18
PUERTO COLLADO TO CASA DE LA MINA AND THE SILK ROUTE ... 116

WALK NO. 19
PUERTO DE FRIGILIANA CIRCUIT ... 121

WALK NO. 20
EL ACEBUCHAL AND CERRO VERDE ... 125

WALK NO. 21
CORTIJO DEL DAIRE AND THE SOUTHERN LUCERO RIDGE 130

WALK NO. 22
THE PEAK OF EL CISNE (THE SWAN) 136

WALK NO. 23
EL ACEBUCHAL TO NERJA VIA PUERTO UMBRALES 141

WALK NO. 24
FRIGILIANA TO THE SUMMIT OF EL FUERTE 145

WALK NO. 25
NERJA TO COLLADO LOS GALGOS VIA THE RÍO CHILLAR 148

WALK NO. 26
MARO VIA EL PINARILLO TO FRIGILIANA OR NERJA 153

WALK NO. 27
FUENTE DEL ESPARTO TO
THE PEAK OF NAVACHICA 158

WALK NO. 28
TAJO EL ALMENDRÓN AND LA PUERTA 162

WALK NO. 29
ASCENT OF EL CIELO 167

WALK NO. 30
THE PEAK OF LA LOPERA 171

El Cisne – WALK 22

ACKNOWLEDGEMENTS

I owe thanks to many of people for enabling me to undertake this project, especially:

- My wife (for putting up with my wanderings).
- My former employers (for sending me to Spain in the first place).
- Spanish Steps (for first getting me involved in guiding).
- Madrid Hash House Harriers (for showing me some wonderful corners of Spain).
- Annette Chalk and John Luffrum (for checking out my walks).
- The owners of these hotels in different parts of Spain, who provide friendship and accommodation for walkers:

Hotel Finca el Cerrillo, Canillas de Albaida (Axarquia)

Hotel Posada la Plaza, Canillas de Albaida (Axarquia)

Hotel Peña Castil, Sotres (Asturias)

Hotel Covadonga, Panes (Asturias)

Hostal Corona, Posada de Valdeon (León)

Hotel Finca Mercedes (La Iruela, Cazorla)

ABOUT SPANISH TRAILS

This is an updated version of Book Two of the Spanish Trails series, providing walks in the Andalucian hills around Cómpeta, and specifically in the natural park of the Sierra Tejeda and Almijara.

Book One of the series covers the Picos de Europa in the north of Spain. Book Three is for the Sierra de Guadarrama, "The Mountains of Madrid". Future editions will cover other parts of Spain.

In principle the books are for hill walkers rather than strollers. However, the walks are graded from easy to strenuous, and hopefully there will be something here for everybody.

CÓMPETA AND THE SIERRA ALMIJARA AND TEJEDA

AN INTRODUCTION

The Axarquia is an area to the east of Málaga. It includes the Parque Natural de las Sierras Almijara y Tejeda, which until relatively recently was hardly known to walkers from outside the region. It is a mountainous area near the south coast of Spain. Within just two or three kilometres of the coastline the land rises to over 500 metres altitude, and there are several summits between 1,500 and 2,000 metres altitude, separated by spectacular ravines and streams. The north-western extreme of the range is the Zafarraya pass, which connects the town of Vélez-Málaga to Alhama de Granada. The south-eastern extreme is where the hills reach the coast to the east of Nerja.

Walking here can be fairly strenuous. Distances are not comparable to similar distances walked in the UK. The hills are steep, and the ground is hard and stony. The paths are mainly ancient mule trails, some of which can be overgrown from lack of use, although many paths have been cleared in recent years by working parties from the local authorities, sometimes by walkers, and by me personally (I have often explored old trails armed with secateurs and shears.) There is nowadays a network of great paths, with spectacular views.

Until the late 1990s hiking was a rare activity in this area, but walking groups from overseas have gradually discovered it. However, some of the more remote peaks remain difficult due to their remoteness, and it is often possible to do a full day's walk here without meeting anybody at all.

This edition focuses on the town of Competa, but the walks can also be accessed from Nerja on the coast, and from

Frigiliana, Canillas de Albaida and Canillas de Aceituno, farther inland.

RECOMMENDED MAPS

There are two 1:25,000 maps covering the area, one for the Sierra Tejeda and the other for the Sierra Almijara. These maps are hard to find outside the local area.

Sierra de Almijara Mapa Topographico
Editor: Miguel Angel Torres Delgado
1:25,000
ISBN: 978-6-99-000431-0, 978-6-99-001961-1 and 978-6-99-000430-3.

The topography in these maps is very good, but they are not as user-friendly as British OS maps, and most footpaths are not marked. You will find it much easier to use the sketch maps I provide with each walk.

A more user-friendly map is the Costa del Sol (Axarquia) Tour and Trail Super-Durable Map
By: David Brawn
1:40,000
ISBN 978-1904946663.

It is available at the time of writing from Stanfords and from Amazon. Some (but not all) of the footpaths are shown. I recommend this map to go alongside my sketch maps.

TRANSPORT

Car hire is very easy from Málaga Airport.

From Málaga take the N340/A7 to the east. For Canillas de Albaida and Cómpeta, leave the motorway at Algarrobo (motorway exit 948) and take the road uphill for about 20 kilometres. For Nerja and Maro, stay on the motorway beyond Algarrobo and follow the signs to Junction 929 or 933 .

There is a bus service from Málaga's central bus station to Nerja (run by ALSA, approximately hourly) and another to Cómpeta and Canillas de Albaida (run by Loymerbus three times daily and twice at weekends). From Málaga to Nerja the trip takes about an hour, and from Málaga to Cómpeta it takes two hours.

ACCOMMODATION

In Competa the main hotel is the Hotel Balcon. There are many hotels and B & Bs in Nerja and Maro. A web search will reveal them. In Canillas de Albaida there are three main choices. In the village centre Posada la Plaza provides reasonably priced accommodation in the heart of the village in a small, rustic hotel with nine bedrooms. It also has a large and comfortable villa capable of accommodating groups of ten to fourteen people. The website www.posada-laplaza.com provides details. The marvellous Hotel Finca el Cerrillo, which is located outside Canillas, offers something really special. See their website at www.hotelfinca.com for further details.

GPS

At the end of each walk description I give a few key GPS references. These are approximate. You must not treat them as exact references. The referencing and the mapping are difficult, due to the complexity of the terrain and some inadequate mapping. You must treat my GPS references as a general guide only.

All my GPS waypoints are stated in accordance with the Spanish grid UTM and Datum WGS84.

Some words of warning:

- GPS signals are erratic or non-existent in some of the valleys.
- Some paper maps and GPS maps show footpaths in

their approximate position. At times you may find yourself walking some 50 metres away from the path shown on the GPS map.
- The presence of a path on a map does not guarantee that it actually exists. It may have been there years ago. Similarly, there are good paths now in existence that are not shown on any published maps.
- My GPS waypoints are in agreement with Garmin's BaseCamp map, but there are discrepancies between these waypoints and the Miguel Angel Torres Delgado maps referred to above. Broadly speaking the eastings are reasonably accurate, but the northings are somewhat inaccurate.

TERMINOLOGY

Spanish	English
Puerto	Mountain pass
Cerro	Hill
Loma	Hillside or bank
Mirador	Viewpoint
Río	River or stream
Fuente	Spring, usually with a tap (untreated hill water)
Cortijo	Farmhouse
Finca	A piece of land (often, but not always, a farm)
Molino	Mill
Fábrica	Factory
Fábrica de la Luz	Former power station

Venta	Inn
Viento	Wind
Vereda	Animal trail
Sendero or Senda	Footpath
Cruz	Cross

GENERAL ADVICE

Since this book is likely to interest regular hill walkers, I will not provide a detailed list of clothing or equipment. But here are some comments.

Although this is southern Spain, which can be sunny and hot, it can rain, and you should carry waterproof clothing in the hills. Generally, lightweight waterproofs will suffice, but bear in mind that in the winter it can be pretty cold at higher levels. For other clothing, lightweight layers are preferable to heavy clothes. Sun protection is essential.

In the winter there can be snow on the higher hills, but it does not stay for long. You would rarely need winter equipment such as crampons.

There are big differences between the seasons. From June to early September it can be very hot. Temperatures can rise to forty degrees in the shade. Summer nights are wonderful, but midsummer is not a good walking season. The best times for walking are from late September through to late May, when temperatures are generally warm but bearable.

There are not many threats to walkers in this region. I don't want to alarm anybody, but I need to mention the following potential dangers:

The processionary caterpillar is poisonous. If you see lines of caterpillars on the ground, or 'cotton wool' nests in pine trees, leave them well alone, as they are dangerous to anybody who may be allergic.

There are snakes, including adders, but they are shy, and rarely seen. Obviously, if you do see one, give it a wide berth.

There are wasps and bees, which can be troublesome but need not worry anybody unless they have a particular allergy.

Hopefully you will not need it, but the international emergency number is 112. If you don't speak Spanish, just say 'English,' and they should put you on to somebody who can help.

THE WALKS

The walks are organised in a roughly geographical sequence, beginning in the north-west of the area and ending in the south-east. I also list the walks in their order of difficulty, and in the walk descriptions I give an idea of the degree of exposure.

You must bear in mind that assessments of difficulty and of exposure are essentially subjective. A difficult walk for one person can be an easy one for another. If you try one of my walks it will help you to judge the remainder.

Each walk has directions, along with a sketch map, which you should use to accompany whichever topographical map you use. The sketch maps are not to exact scale, but they are generally speaking drawn from my own GPS tracks.

Some of the walks may cover some of the same ground as in other walks. Sometimes, but not always, this will be in the opposite direction. However, where there is an overlap, it is in order to provide a different overall route.

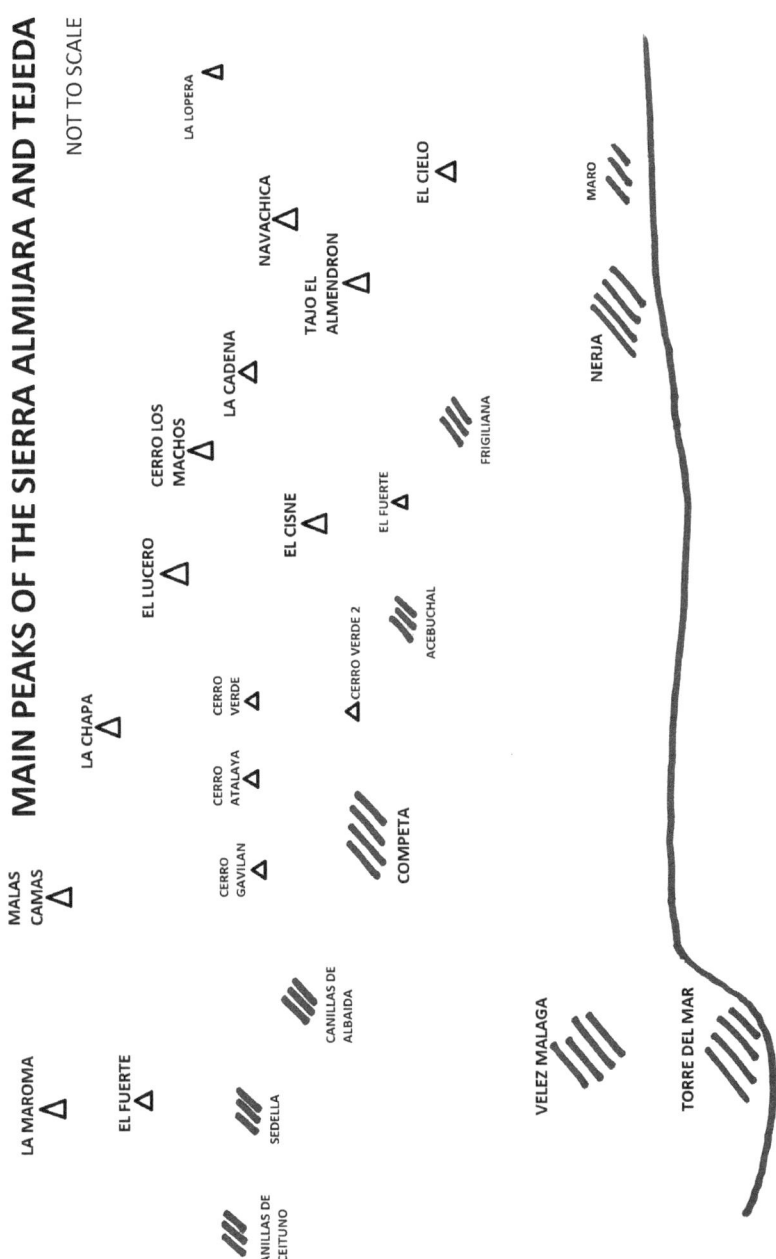

THE WALKS IN ORDER OF DIFFICULTY

In the main index, which follows this one, the walks are numbered in a geographical sequence, beginning in the north-western corner of the sierra and ending in the south-east.

That index shows the approximate distances involved, along with an estimate of the total ascent in metres and the perceived degree of difficulty and exposure.

The following index shows the walks in the order of difficulty that I have given to them:

Walk 27	Fuente del Esparto to the peak of Navachica	Very strenuous
Walk 15	El Lucero from La Fábrica de la Luz	Very strenuous
Walk 28	Tajo del Almendrón and La Puerta	Very strenuous
Walk 3	La Maroma circuit from Canillas de Aceituno	Very strenuous
Walk 14	Malas Camas from La Fábrica	Very strenuous
Walk 16	El Lucero circuit from Puerto Blanquillo	Strenuous
Walk 1	Ascent of La Maroma from Canillas de Aceituno	Strenuous
Walk 9	Canillas de Albaida to Salares circuit	Strenuous
Walk 19	Puerto de Frigiliana circuit	Strenuous
Walk 22	The peak of El Cisne	Strenuous
Walk 23	El Acebuchal to Nerja via Puerto Umbrales	Strenuous
Walk 29	Ascent of El Cielo	Strenuous

Walk 26	Maro via El Pinarillo to Nerja or Frigiliana	Strenuous
Walk 20	El Acebuchal and Cerro Verde	Strenuous
Walk 4	Almanchares ravine and the hanging bridge	Moderate to strenuous
Walk 21	Cortijo del Daire and the southern Lucero ridge	Moderate to strenuous
Walk 7	Sedella to Los Picaricos	Moderate to strenuous
Walk 13	La Fábrica to Cerro Verde and Cerro Atalaya	Moderate to Strenuous
Walk 2	La Maroma from Los Llanos de Sedella	Moderate
Walk 17	The Silk Route and La Fábrica	Moderate
Walk 5	Sedella to Canillas de Aceituno	Moderate
Walk 9**	Canillas de Albaida to Salares one way	Moderate
Walk 10	Canillas de Albaida to Cerro Gavilán	Moderate
Walk 11	Casa de la Mina circuit	Moderate
Walk 8	Canillas de Albaida to Sedella	Moderate
Walk 6	Sedella to El Fuerte	Moderate
Walk 18	Puerto Collado to Casa de la Mina and the Silk Route	Moderate
Walk 25	Nerja to Los Galgos via el Río Chillar	Moderate
Walk 12	Cómpeta and the three villages walk	Moderate
Walk 24	Frigiliana to the summit of El Fuerte	Easy
Walk 30	The peak of La Lopera	Easy

THE SIERRA ALMIJARA AND TEJEDA

SKETCH MAP OF WALK LOCATIONS

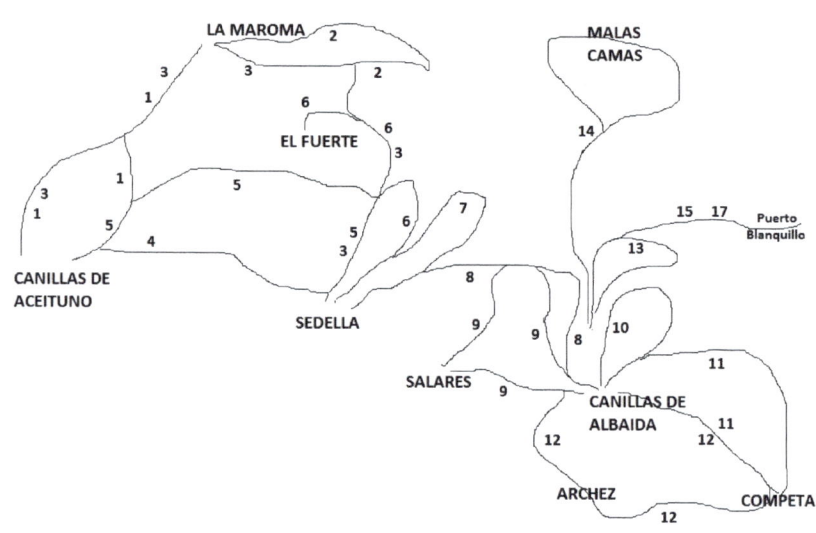

Not to scale: *it is just intended to show the location of each walk in relation to each of the others.*

La Maroma from El Cisne - **Walk 22**

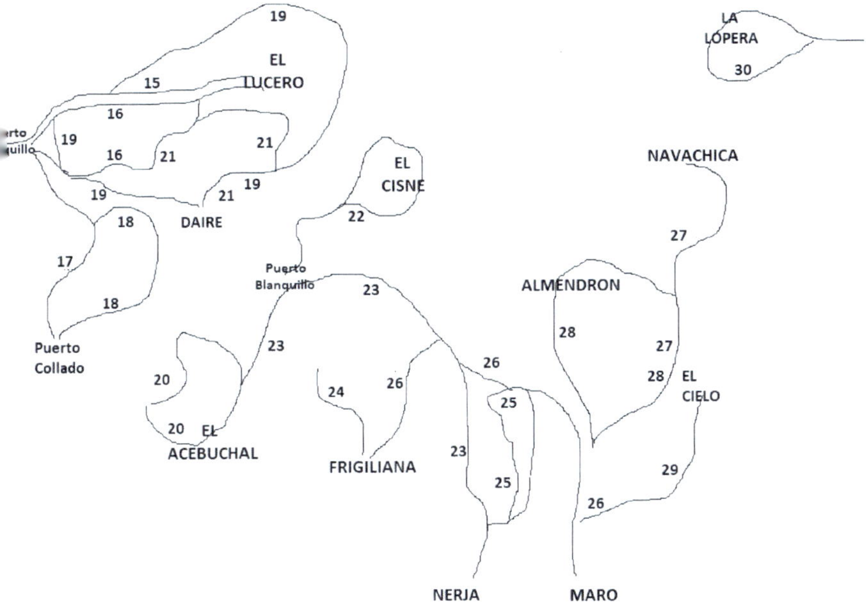

PHIL LAWLER

```
                                                          LA
                      19                                  LOPERA
                      EL
                      LUCERO                                30
             15
          16
 rto   19                   21                                      NAVACHICA
uillo     16    21     21
       19          19                    EL
          18              21             CISNE
    17         DAIRE                                                    27
                          Puerto                    ALMENDRON
          18              Blanquillo  22
                                        23                  28
 Puerto                                                              27
 Collado                                                                  EL
                    20           23           26      28                  CIELO
                                     26              25
                           24
                 20    EL                                             29
                    ACEBUCHAL            23
                          FRIGILIANA
                                              25
                                                     26


                                 NERJA            MARO
```

View towards Sierra Nevada - **Walks 15 & 16**

WALKS IN THE AXARQUIA

WALK NO.	ROUTE	DISTANCE (kms)	ASCENT (metres)
1 - Strenuous	Ascent of La Maroma from Canillas de Aceituno	20	1,500

DESCRIPTION: *The highest point in the area*

2 - Moderate	La Maroma from Los Llanos de Sedella	12	650

DESCRIPTION: *Starts at high level but needs a four-wheel drive*

3 - Very Strenuous	La Maroma circuit from Canillas de Aceituno	22	1,500

DESCRIPTION: *Ascent to and traverse of the summit, descending to another nearby village*

4 - Moderate to strenuous	Almanchares ravine and the hanging bridge ("Puente Colgante")	11 linear	800

DESCRIPTION: *Village to village, crossing a suspended footbridge. Not for vertigo sufferers.*

5 - Moderate	Sedella to Canillas de Aceituno	12 linear	825

DESCRIPTION: *A traverse below the south face of La Maroma*

6 - Moderate	Sedella to El Fuerte	12	700

DESCRIPTION: *Ascent to a minor peak below La Maroma*

7 - Moderate to strenuous	Sedella to Los Picaricos	11	700

DESCRIPTION: *A walk to a remote ruined farm. More than moderate, due to overgrown paths and steepness*

8 - Moderate	Canillas de Albaida to Sedella	13 linear	640

DESCRIPTION: *From one White Town of Andalucia to another*

9 - Strenuous or moderate	Canillas de Albaida to Salares	16 circular or 10 linear	800 or 530

DESCRIPTION: *From one White Town of Andalucia to another*

10 - Moderate	Canillas de Albaida to Cerro Gavilán	12	650

DESCRIPTION: *Ascent to a fire watch station on a hilltop*

11 - Moderate	Casa de la Mina circuit	15	710

DESCRIPTION: *Ascent and traverse to a remote hotel and landmark*

12 - Moderate	Cómpeta and the three villages walk	12	650

DESCRIPTION: *A circuit of Cómpeta, Canillas and Árchez*

13 - Moderate to Strenuous	La Fábrica to Cerro Verde and Cerro Atalaya	13	800

DESCRIPTION: *Ascent to two intermediate peaks*

14 - Very Strenuous	Malas Camas from La Fábrica	20	1,250

DESCRIPTION: *Ascent to a little-visited high peak*

| 15 - Very Strenuous | El Lucero from La Fábrica de la Luz | 22 round trip | 1,400 |

DESCRIPTION: *Ascent to the area's most emblematic peak*

| 16 - Very Strenuous | El Lucero circuit from Puerto Blanquillo | 13 | 950 |

DESCRIPTION: *Ascent to the area's most attractive peak, returning via a spectacular and more difficult route*

| 17 - Moderate | The Silk Route and La Fábrica | 14 linear | 570 |

DESCRIPTION: *A linear walk along the area's old 'main road', the ancient mule trail towards Granada*

| 18 - Moderate | Puerto Collado to Casa la Mina and the Silk Route | 14 | 450 |

DESCRIPTION: *A circuit including part of the Silk Route in reverse direction from Walk 17*

| 19 - Strenuous | Puerto de Frigiliana circuit | 17.5 | 1,050 |

DESCRIPTION: *A circuit from the El Daire ruin via Puerto de Frigiliana and the northern side of El Lucero*

| 20 - Strenuous | El Acebuchal and Cerro Verde | 17 | 660 |

DESCRIPTION: *A circular route from near Cómpeta via the remote hamlet of El Acebuchal*

| 21 - Moderate to Strenuous | Cortijo del Daire and the southern Lucero ridge | 9 or 19 | 800 or 1,500 |

DESCRIPTION: *Two possible routes to the old ruined inn of El Daire and the isolated southern slopes of El Lucero*

| 22 - Strenuous | The peak of El Cisne | 9.5 | 915 |

DESCRIPTION: *A remote and spectacular mountain with two peaks*

| 23 - Strenuous | El Acebuchal to Nerja via Puerto Umbrales | 18 or 20 linear | 850 or 1,200 |

DESCRIPTION: *A linear walk through high mountain passes and river valleys to the coast*

| 24 - Easy | Frigiliana to the summit of El Fuerte | 9 round trip | 730 |

DESCRIPTION: *From the lovely village of Frigiliana to the summit of the hill that overlooks it*

| 25 - Moderate | Nerja to Collado Los Galgos via the Río Chillar | 17 | 950 |

DESCRIPTION: *River valleys, broad ridges, remote landscapes and good views*

| 26 - Strenuous | Maro via El Pinarillo to Frigiliana or Nerja | 15 or 18 | 950 or 1,000 |

DESCRIPTION: *From near the coast to Frigiliana or Nerja via high ridges and stream valleys*

| 27 - Very Strenuous | Fuente del Esparto to the peak of Navachica | 8.5 each way | 1,350 |

DESCRIPTION: *A tough ascent to the highest point in the Sierra Almijara (1,832 metres)*

| 28 - Very Strenuous | Tajo del Almendrón and La Puerta | 15 | 1,050 |

DESCRIPTION: *A circular route to a brilliant viewpoint and peak*

| 29 - Strenuous | Ascent of El Cielo | 7 each way | 1,250 |

DESCRIPTION: *Ascent of the peak overlooking the coast near Nerja*

| 30 - Easy | The peak of La Lopera | 9 | 320 |

DESCRIPTION: *A circular route to an easy peak with good views. On the way to Granada*

Slopes of La Maroma - WALK 1

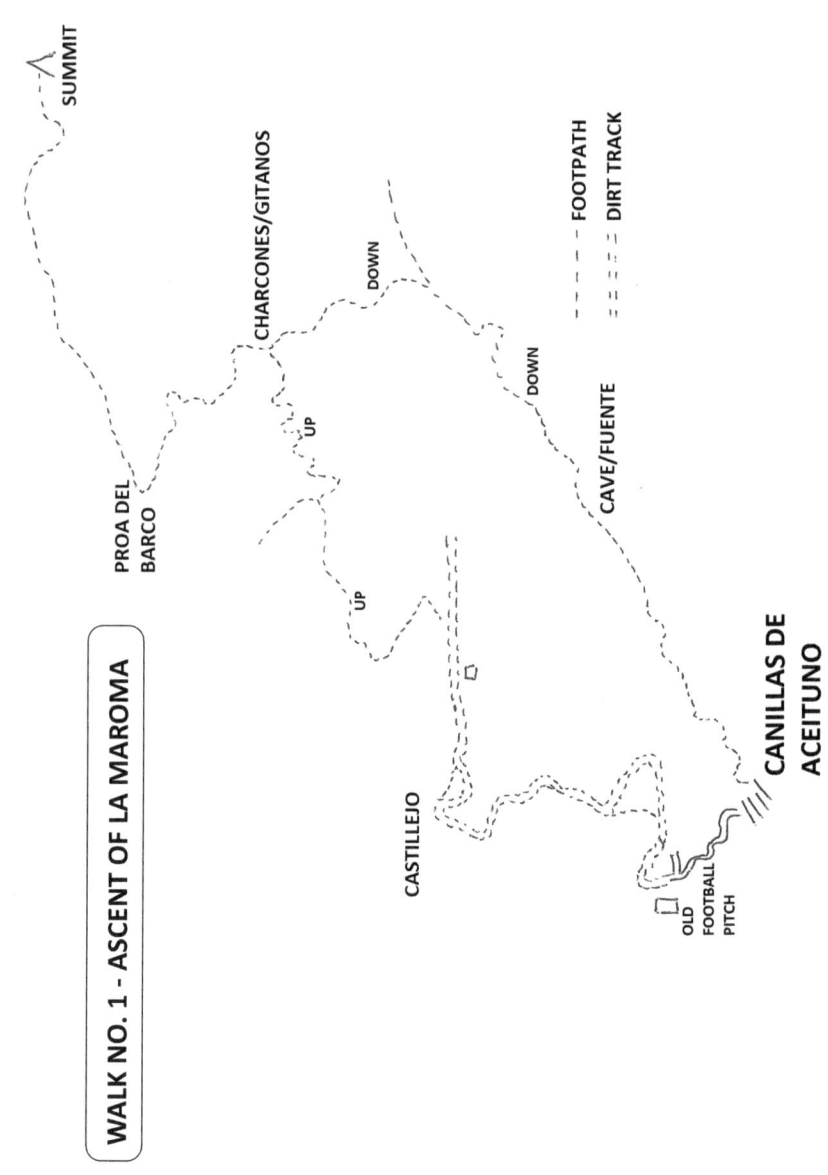

WALK NO. 1

ASCENT OF LA MAROMA FROM CANILLAS DE ACEITUNO

The classic ascent of the highest peak in the province of Málaga.

Distance	20 km
Ascent	1,500 metres
Overall grade	Strenuous
Terrain	Tracks, footpaths and limestone pavement
Exposure	None
Highest point	2,069 metres

The walk begins and ends in the village of Canillas de Aceituno.

- Walk up some steps to the left side of the *ayuntamiento* (town hall) of Canillas de Aceituno, and turn left on a lane, with a signpost for La Maroma. At the top of the slope, where some streets go up to the right, keep straight ahead. Ignore any further signposts for La Maroma, and instead follow a concrete road ahead to walk uphill to the right of the cemetery. Carry on – still uphill – on a dirt track, and walk past an old, disused football pitch. Ignore a broad track going to the right before you reach the football pitch. And do not go to the smart new football pitch below the village. Look for the old one, which is higher up, to the north-west of the village.

- After the football pitch follow the track as it bends sharp right. Then, after about 250 metres, take a footpath going uphill to the left. It cuts off some long bends and joins the dirt track once more, at a point where two other footpaths start. But ignore these footpaths. Instead go along the main track, gently uphill. Almost 1 kilometre after rejoining the track you will reach a sharp right-hand bend, and there are rocks ahead of you with a great view down into the valley below. This is known as the Castillejo. Turn right here. But, instead of staying on the track, take a path uphill, which cuts out some bends.

- On joining the track once more turn left along it. On a level stretch you will pass a building on the right. A little further on take a path going downhill to the left, where a big signpost points to La Maroma. The path descends to pass an old limepit. Then follow the path as it winds its way uphill, now heading towards the north-west. It leads you into the next valley, swings to the north-east, and, still ascending, reaches a narrow watercourse. But a few metres before the watercourse, at a small cairn, turn uphill to the right. (The path is marked with a post and an arrow.)

- At this point the path can be somewhat overgrown, so keep a keen eye open so you don't lose the path. It continues uphill in zigzags, sometimes quite steeply, to reach a T-junction of paths at rocky outcrops known as El Collado de Los Gitanos (the Gipsies' Col). This is shown as Los Charcones on some maps. Turn left and follow the path on the level at first, turn left to cross a watercourse, and continue uphill once more. Follow the path upwards, often in more zigzags, until you reach a rocky area with a bare limestone hill ahead, and a big view down on your left. This is the Proa del Barco (the Ship's Prow). The path turns sharp right here – almost back on itself – over rocky ground, and is marked with cairns.

- Follow the cairns going north-east, and keep to the right of a valley bottom. You will gradually ascend, but the valley bottom comes up to meet you. Follow the cairns, which you will see are now in the centre of the valley, and pass near some rocky outcrops on the right. (The second of these has a lovely grassy area below it, making a great resting place.) The summit is ahead, although the very top is still out of sight. The route is marked with cairns. It goes diagonally to the right, ascending the hill. Swing to the left as you reach the crest of the hill to complete the ascent to the summit.

- At the summit you will see a navigation tower, and there are several windbreaks for picnics. There is a deep pothole about 50 metres to the south-west from the summit. The summit is a wide plateau on which there are at least four tops. No matter which of the tops you stand on, the others look higher. I would not like to definitively state which is the highest.

- From the summit, retrace your steps along the outward route to the Proa del Barco and continue downhill to the Collado de los Gitanos. But here, instead of turning right to follow the route of ascent, go to the left across a rocky area and then follow the path downhill.

- The path heads south-east and crosses the head of a valley. You will then begin walking downhill again, to the south. Ignore a path that comes in from below on the left, and continue descending the hillside of La Rábita in a south-westerly direction. Pass a small cave, just beyond which there is a *fuente* (a spring), and then you will cross a big slab of white limestone. The path starts again at the bottom left-hand side of the rocky slab.

- Follow this path as it descends through pinewoods all the way back to Canillas de Aceituno. At the top of the village you will reach a dirt track. Turn right and walk along it for 50 metres. Then go left to pass immediately by some farm buildings and then down some steps with a fence alongside them to return to the village centre.

WALK NO. 1

APPROXIMATE GPS REFERENCES (UTM)

Start and finish	403467 4081507
Old football pitch	403214 4082000
Castillejo	403518 4082885
El Collado de Los Gitanos	405604 4083567
Proa del Barco	404986 4084202
Summit	406849 4084586
La Rábita	405651 4082583
Fuente	404981 4082236

On the descent of La Maroma - **WALK 1**

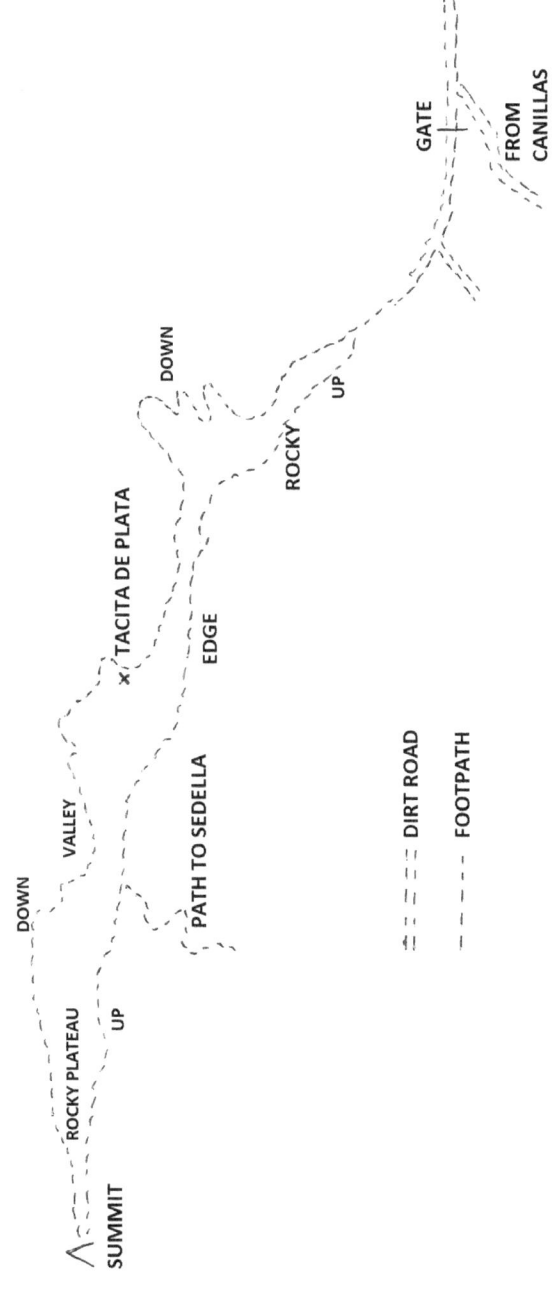

WALK NO. 2

LA MAROMA FROM LOS LLANOS DE SEDELLA

A shorter route to the summit of La Maroma, but requiring a four-wheel drive to reach the start of the walk. (In a saloon car or you may well ground it.)

Distance	12 km
Ascent	650 metres
Overall grade	Moderate
Terrain	Footpaths, limestone pavement and bare rock
Exposure	Minimal
Highest point	2,069 metres

To reach the start of the walk:

Drive on a dirt track from the village of Salares towards Fogarate. To find the track, coming from Sedella, take the left fork at the top of a hill as you reach the outskirts of Salares. The dirt track is then the first turning on the left.

Stay on this track for about 4 kilometres. On the way you will pass a goat shed on the right, and then a water tank on a bend. Soon you will cross a bridge where the track swings right, and at the top of an incline another track goes down to the right. Stay on the main track, but take the next track uphill to the left. There may be a sign forbidding motorbikes.

You now have a long drive uphill on a rough, zigzagging track. On the way, ignore a track going left. At the next junction turn left. Fork right at the following junction, and keep to the better track. Pass through a makeshift gate and at a T-junction on the ridge turn left, then park by a gateway. This area is known as Los Llanos de Sedella.

THE WALK:

- Walk through the gate, going west, and continue along the dirt track until it comes to an end. A vague path goes towards the mountain. Your aim is to ascend the rocky ridge ahead and then keep as close as reasonably possible to its left-hand edge, with views to the south practically all the way. When you reach the first rocks you will see a good path going away to the right. Ignore it. It is the return route. Instead, go upwards on loose, stony ground up a small gully. Continue over several rocky rises, descending a little at times. The path soon becomes more evident, and there are occasional cairns and splashes of red paint. If in doubt keep to the high ground near the left (southern) edge of the plateau, although at times there is a good path below the crest on the northern slopes.

- Having gone past several rocky tops, and keeping close to the edge, you will reach an area where a valley with trees descends to your right. The path then ascends once more, still keeping close to the south face. At this point there is a precipice below to your left, but there is ample room to avoid it on the right. However, the route is somewhat airy and may not suit anybody with real vertigo.

- At this point, about 3.5 km into the walk, a path descends down the south face to the left. This is a good route to Sedella, but you should ignore it for this walk. The correct path leaves the southerly face of the mountain and starts to ascend to the right in zigzags, then goes just north of west. Follow the cairns. Soon you will be walking over smooth limestone, with loose stones dotted about. The route will take you over some false summits until you reach the tower at the official summit of La Maroma.

- There is a deep pothole 50 metres below the summit to the south-west, which you may care to look down. It was fenced off in early 2015. The mountain has several summits, all of a similar height, although, strangely, from each of them the others appear higher.

- To continue this circuit go north-east from the tower to the next summit, then on to the third one. And then, shortly before the last summit, look for a wooden marker post a little to the right. Go to this post, which marks the way up from the north side of the mountain. Try to follow the wooden markers down a very rough and intermittent path as you pick your way down the stony hill. The general direction is now south-east. Take care near the foot of the hill, as there are some rough limestone rocks to be circumnavigated.

- You will reach a depression where there are fenced areas and trees to the right. The path crosses above a gully where another path descends to the left (north). This is the Salto del Caballo (the Horse's Leap). Cross above the gully and follow the path up the other side. It swings right, and before a fenced area a path goes up to the left. Follow this path, passing close to and high above the gully, which is below on the left. The path then swings to the right, passing round the end of the hill. The path improves from here on. As you are heading south, above you to the right, near some pine trees, there is a very small spring. This is the Tacita de Plata (the Little Silver Cup).

- When you look ahead from here you should see the path going to the left across the opposite hillside. With the Tacita de Plata spring behind you, continue to the south over a rocky path in slight descent. Then cross a dry watercourse and pick up that path to the left. It takes you back towards the ridge you ascended earlier. On reaching it take a path to the left below the top of the ridge. It now goes to the north for a while.

- As you round the end of a hill you will see a good path below to the left. Descend the slope and pick up this path. It then reaches a small col where a clear path descends to the right and goes in big zigzags downhill, passing a spring where a goatherd uses a bath to collect water. Stay on this path until it takes you slightly uphill to reach a grassy area and the small dirt track you walked along at the start of the walk. Follow the track back to your car.

APPROXIMATE GPS REFERENCES (UTM)

Start and finish	410969 4083165
On the ridge	409145 4084211
Top of path to Sedella	408193 4084454
La Maroma summit	406849 4084568
On the descent	408151 4084677
Salto del Caballo	408556 4084584
Tacita de Plata	409000 4084462
Keep left	409365 4084231
The zigzags	409919 4084190

WALK NO. 3

WALK NO. 3 - LA MAROMA – CIRCUIT FROM CANILLAS DE ACEITUNO

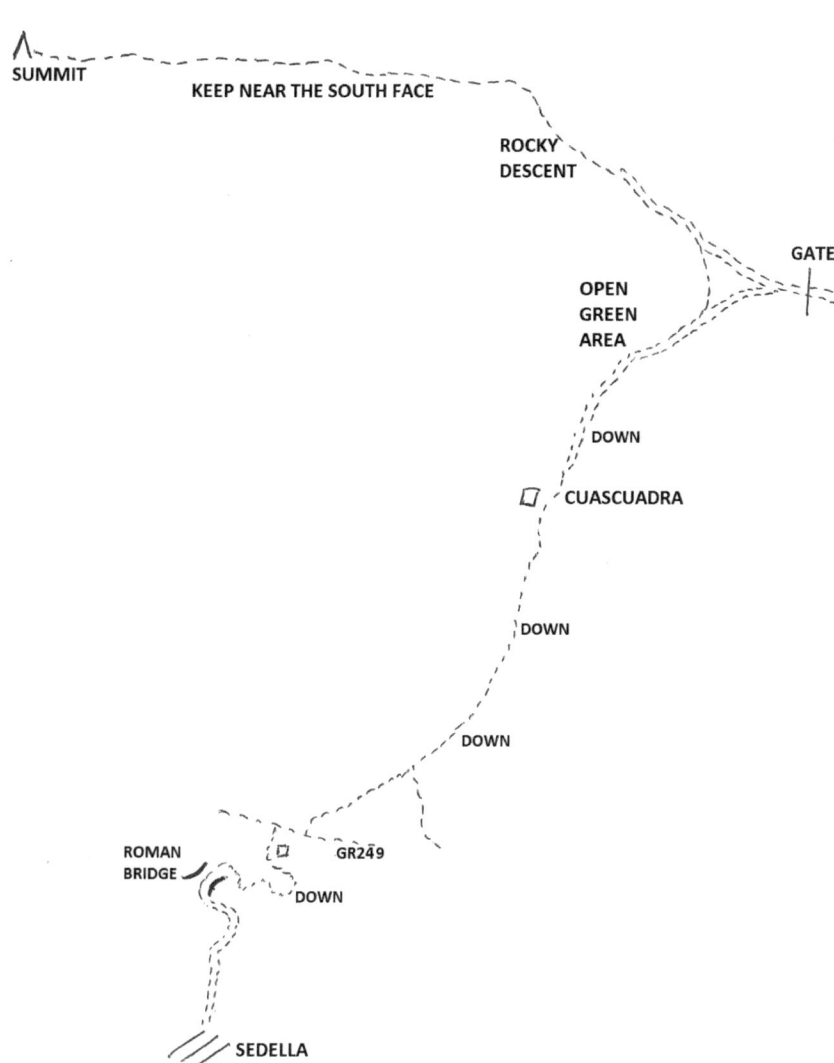

WALK NO. 3

LA MAROMA – CIRCUIT FROM CANILLAS DE ACEITUNO

Distance	22 km
Ascent	1,500 metres
Overall grade	Very Strenuous
Terrain	Tracks, footpaths and limestone pavement
Exposure	Minimal
Highest point	2,069 metres

This route follows the ascent of La Maroma described in Walk 1, then goes along the summit plateau to the east, descending via a little-used mule trail to Sedella (22 km). You will need to arrange transport for the few kilometres back to the start. If you have two cars leave one at each end.

- From Canillas de Aceituno follow the route set out in Walk 1 (Ascent of La Maroma from Canillas de Aceituno). It should take you around four hours to reach the summit.

- At the tower on the summit plateau look for a line of cairns leading across the slope, going slightly to the south of east. The route/path gradually descends across bare limestone, staying high above the south face of the mountain. Keep a keen eye open for the cairns, which are intermittent and can be difficult to spot. This stretch is very difficult in mist, so *I recommend this route for clear days only*.

- You will descend along the shoulder of the dome-shaped rocky plateau. The path soon descends more steeply, in zigzags. It leads close to the edge of the precipice on the south face of the mountain, but there is ample room to stay away from the very edge. *Approximately 1.25 kilometres from the summit, a path goes down to the right, below the south face. This path leads to Sedella, but the walk described here takes a longer route. If you decide to take the shorter route, see the alternative route described below (1).*

- This route stays higher for longer and follows an ancient route that is rarely used, and is therefore partially overgrown. You may scratch your legs if walking in shorts. On the descent from the summit, after about 1.25 km, ignore the path going down to Sedella. Instead, continue along intermittent paths leading you over and around rocky ground, but always keeping near the right-hand (south) side of the plateau. At a point where the ridge separates into two ridges, keep to the right-hand one and stay high. After a short descent over loose stones you will emerge on to an open area of grassy meadows, often with goats or cattle present.

- Having left the rocks behind, take the dirt track leading to the east. Leave it before reaching a gate in a fence and cross the grassy area on the right, to follow a track going south-west. The track follows the top of a broad green ridge and leads down to a semi-ruined *venta* (an inn) called Cuascuadra. You may meet horses, which are stabled here. From Cuascuadra a path continues down the nose of the ridge, becoming sandy and loose in places, and sometimes very steep.

- About 1.5 km from Cuascuadra, after a loss of about 350 metres altitude, you will reach an area where a valley opens up before you. Go to the right across scrubby ground towards the western side of the valley. Keep descending to find a footpath, which will lead you to a level area where the signposted footpath GR 249 crosses your path. Turn right along it for about 100 metres, and then descend to the left over rough ground to reach the disused goat shed of La Herreriza.

- A large cairn below the goat shed marks the start of a stony path to the right, going down to the Roman Bridge of Sedella, from where it is a stroll along a broad track into the village of Sedella.

APPROXIMATE GPS REFERENCES (UTM)

Start	403467 4081507
Summit	406849 4084568

MAIN ROUTE:	
Top of 'alternative' path	408193 4084454
On the ridge	409145 4084211
Top of path	410592 4083236
Cuascuadra	409681 4082308
Keep right	409047 4081220
GR 249	408617 4080990
La Herreriza	408531 4080767

ALTERNATIVE:	
Top of path	408193 4084454
Col near El Fuerte	407433 4083261
Clearing	407394 4082355
Area recreativa	407039 4080949

ALTERNATIVE DESCENT
(DESCENT TO THE AREA RECREATIVA OF SEDELLA)

- Descending from the summit to the east, after about 1.25 km you will see a broad gully coming up from the right, with a path going down the far side of the gully. This is the way down to the *area recreativa*, or picnic area, of Sedella.

- Take this path down into the gully. The ground is loose, and the condition of the path has deteriorated recently. To add to the difficulties it is also steep at certain points, so walking poles are very helpful. But there is no real exposure, despite first appearances.

- The path zigzags repeatedly, and can be difficult to find at times. It eventually crosses from the eastern side of the broad gully to the far side, and then ascends to reach a ridge going towards the hill of El Fuerte (which is the subject of a separate walk in this collection). Keep to the path at all times. After having conquered a minor summit and skirted to the west of another one, you will arrive at a col directly below the top of El Fuerte.

- At the col the path swings sharply downhill to the left in zigzags, and then takes a straighter route to lead downhill past a *fuente* (a water source). Shortly afterwards it reaches a level clearing where a signpost shows the way back up to La Maroma. At the clearing ignore the sharp turn to the left and take the next track on the left instead. Follow the main broad dirt track downhill to the right (south). Stay on this dirt track all the way down, ignoring one turn-off to the left, to reach the hut of La Choza del Guarda. Go to the right here, turn left at the next junction, and go downhill to reach the *area recreativa* (a picnic and barbecue area) above Sedella, from where you will need transport.

PUENTE COLGANTE

WALK NO. 4 - PUENTE COLGANTE/ HANGING BRIDGE

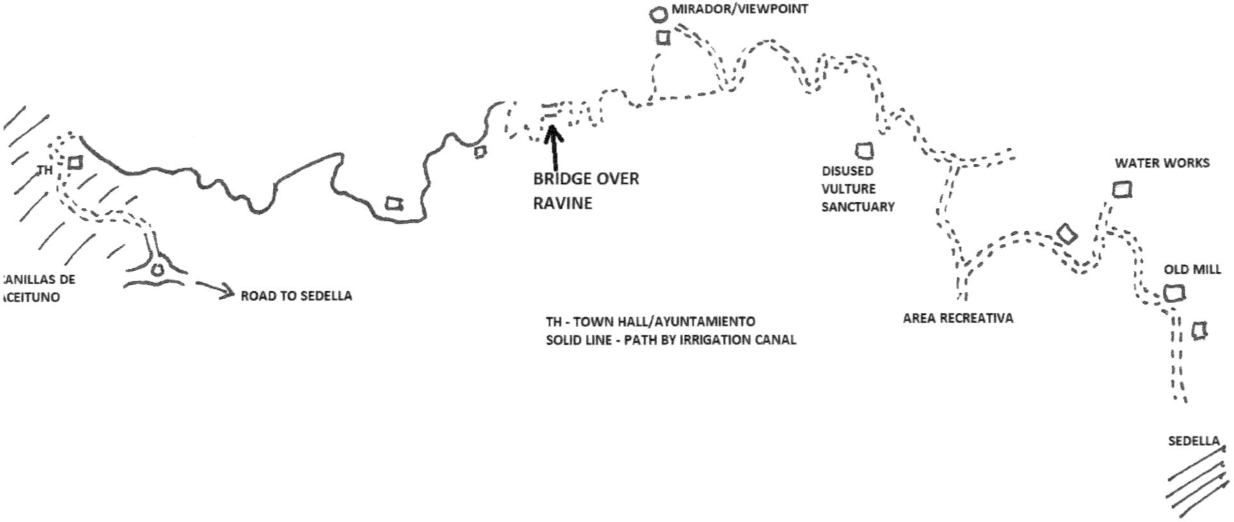

- WATER WORKS
- OLD MILL
- SEDELLA
- AREA RECREATIVA
- DISUSED VULTURE SANCTUARY
- MIRADOR/VIEWPOINT
- BRIDGE OVER RAVINE
- TH - TOWN HALL/AYUNTAMIENTO
- SOLID LINE - PATH BY IRRIGATION CANAL
- ROAD TO SEDELLA
- ANILLAS DE CEITUNO
- TH

Bridge over the Almanchares – **WALK 4**

WALK NO. 4

PUENTE COLGANTE (THE HANGING BRIDGE)

A linear walk from Canillas de Aceituno to Sedella, crossing a suspended bridge over the Almanchares ravine.

The walk follows part of the long-distance path GR249, so is generally well signposted. This section of the GR249 was created in about 2021, when the bridge was built.

Distance	11 kms
Ascent	800 metres
Overall grade	Moderate to Strenuous
Terrain	Level walking alongside an irrigation canal, then a steep descent, a somewhat vertiginous hanging bridge and a steep ascent. Finally, good broad tracks
Exposure	Very little if care is taken. But the area around the bridge and the crossing itself require a reasonable head for heights.

Vertigo sufferers may not want to cross the hanging bridge. However, they can do the first part of the walk, see the ravine, and then return to the start. It is still a very worthwhile walk

- Start the walk in Canillas de Aceituno. Face the town hall (the *ayuntamiento*) then go up some steps to its left and turn left following a sign for La Maroma. Take an uphill turn to the right, and ascend through narrow, twisting streets to a point near the highest part of the village, where a set of steps leads up to a goat shed. (You should find occasional signs pointing the way up through the village). After leaving the houses and before reaching the top of the steps, take a footpath going off to the right, next to a signpost for the Gran Senda de Malaga (the GR249)

- The path follows the line of an *acequia* (an irrigation canal). (The water is now mainly contained within a pipeline). Soon you will reach an open water tank, and the path continues beyond it, ascending towards another *acequia* at a higher level.

- The path crosses a broad gully and then continues past a ruined farm on the left. Keep going, more or less on the level, until you reach a hut. Continue on the path. You will soon reach a fence above the sheer wall of the Almanchares ravine. A recently built (2017) section of fenced metal walkway leads along the cliff face for a short distance, and the unfenced *acequia* path then continues. Shortly before a second fenced walkway begins, take a steep path downhill to the right into the ravine. You will see the impressive bridge below. The descent is fairly vertiginous, but the path is a good one and well used, so it presents no technical difficulty.

- Cross the bridge. It is well protected and safe to cross, but the authorities have imposed a limit of 10 people to be on the bridge at any one time. It wobbles slightly as you cross it.

- At the far end of the bridge a footpath goes very steeply uphill on the eastern side of the ravine. There are chains at times to hold on to if you need them. This section is not technically difficult but it is very steep and a fall would not be advisable, so take care. (It is far better to ascend this section than to descend it).

- At the top of the hill (an ascent of about 200 metres) you will cross a green area and reach a broad track. Turn left here to reach the viewpoint Mirador de los Pozuelos, with a great view of La Maroma above and the Almanchares ravine below.

PUENTE COLGANTE

- Leave the Mirador and follow the broad track to the east. The walking is now easy. You will pass an old lime pit and a wooden structure, which was a sanctuary for vultures when the authorities were encouraging the reintroduction of wildlife.

- At a junction of tracks turn right and descend to reach the Area Recreativa de Sedella, with its statue of an ibex. Before the statue turn left on a track which takes you to a large goat farm. Beyond it go left round a bend and then sharp right to reach an old water mill. From the mill take the track going south, which leads through olive and almond groves and irrigated terraces to reach the village of Sedella.

APPROXIMATE GPS REFERENCES (UTM)

Start	403549 4081337
Start of acequia path	403642 4081522
The hut	405172 4081482
Los Saltillos	405807 4082026
Mirador de los Pozuelos	405867 4081828
Go left (east)	407046 4081011
Water mill (Molino)	407689 4080885

South Lucero Ridge – **WALK 21**

WALK NO. 5

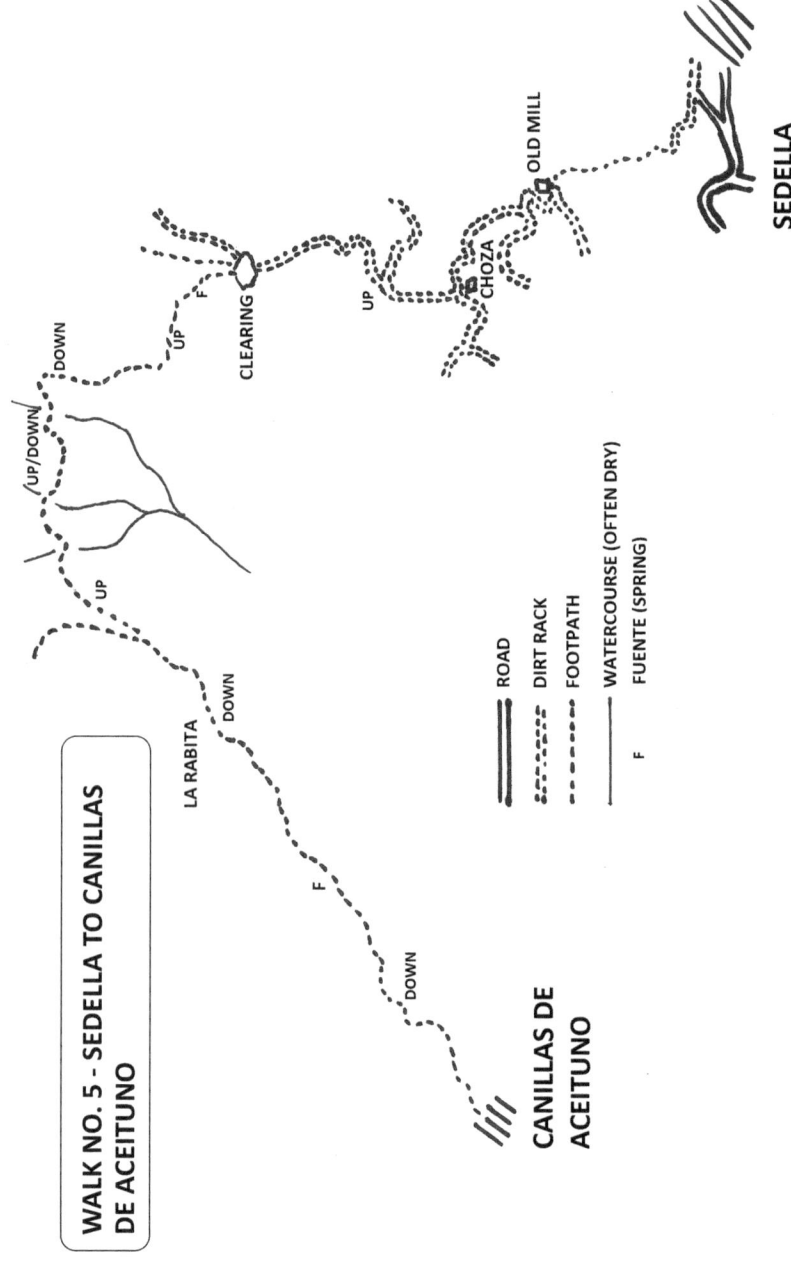

WALK NO. 5

SEDELLA TO CANILLAS DE ACEITUNO

A linear walk with a transport requirement. It can be made into a circular route by returning to the start using Walk 4 of this book. This makes for a strenuous day.

Some of the early stages of this walk follow the route towards El Fuerte (Walk 6).

Distance	12 km one way
Ascent	825 metres
Overall grade	Moderate
Terrain	Tracks and footpaths
Exposure	None
Highest point	1,314 metres

- From the bus stop at the western end of Sedella, walk into the village, past the *fuente* (water taps) and an old wash house, and then past Bar Lorena on the left. Take the very next turning left, ascend some steps, and turn left along a track, which has a signpost saying *Canillas de Aceituno 8.5 km* (but this route to Canillas de Aceituno is longer than 8.5 km and is more interesting).

- After just a few metres the track swings to the right. Follow it uphill through irrigated farm terraces, where you will pass by alternate olive and almond groves. It will soon lead you to the old water-driven flour mill of Sedella. It is preserved as a local monument. When you are facing the mill take the track to the left, and then almost immediately turn right uphill on another track. At this moment you will be on the signposted route GR 249. Follow it to the top of a small ridge, where the marked route turns left. However, you should turn right instead, going slightly uphill.

- Go along a broad track, crossing a chain, and continue as it goes to the left. It leads you soon to La Choza del Guarda, an old but reconstructed shelter. (Here the route joins Walk 6 for a time.) Turn right here, and follow the main track gradually uphill. There is one junction, where a minor track goes to the right. But keep left and stay on the main track until you reach a broad, flat clearing on the left.

- At the clearing, another minor track goes to the right and a signpost indicates a footpath to the top of La Maroma. Ignore both of those, and instead cross the clearing going to the west, beyond the sign for La Maroma. At the far right-hand corner of the clearing take another path to the right, more or less on the level at first, but soon ascending towards a limestone outcrop that stands out ahead. The path goes towards the top of this limestone outcrop, near a *fuente* (a spring), but do not rely on it because it can dry up. The path swings right and then left again just before the *fuente*, and continues to ascend, passing above the limestone outcrop. Follow the path upwards. There are no alternatives – although you need to look out for zigzags, which you can miss at times in the undergrowth.

- The path leads to a col, from where you can see down into the Almanchares ravine at a higher level than the one described in Walk 4. Keep to the path, which swings to the right here, and then begins a zigzag descent into the upper reaches of the ravine. This is remote and wild country, and the path can become overgrown with rosemary and gorse. Keep a close eye open so as not to lose the path. The the only living things you are likely to meet are *cabra montés* (ibex) or wild boar (the boar are nocturnal, so encounters are rare).

- Continue down to cross the watercourse (which is usually dry), then ascend to a col. From here you will descend, to cross another watercourse, and then you will ascend once more. Don't start celebrating yet – it happens again. After the third crossing you will ascend in earnest, and soon reach the path which connects Canillas de Aceituno to La Maroma. Turn left on this path, along the hillside of La Rábita, and descend all the way to the village.

- The descent on this path is the same as the final part of Walk 1. On the way you will pass by some bare landscape, which shows the serious effects of wildfire. Pass a small cave and then a *fuente* (a spring) and cross a white limestone 'platform', from the far bottom left corner of which the path continues down. Just outside the village you will reach a track by some pylons. Go to the right on the track and turn left immediately in front of a goat shed, where a path leads you down steps and into the village.

APPROXIMATE GPS REFERENCES (UTM)

Start	407677 4080158
Water mill	407689 4080885
Chozo del Guarda	407109 4081240
Clearing	407394 4082355
Watercourse	406770 4083250
Junction	405856 4082929
Fuente	404981 4082236

WALK NO. 6

WALK NO. 6 - SEDELLA TO THE SUMMIT OF EL FUERTE

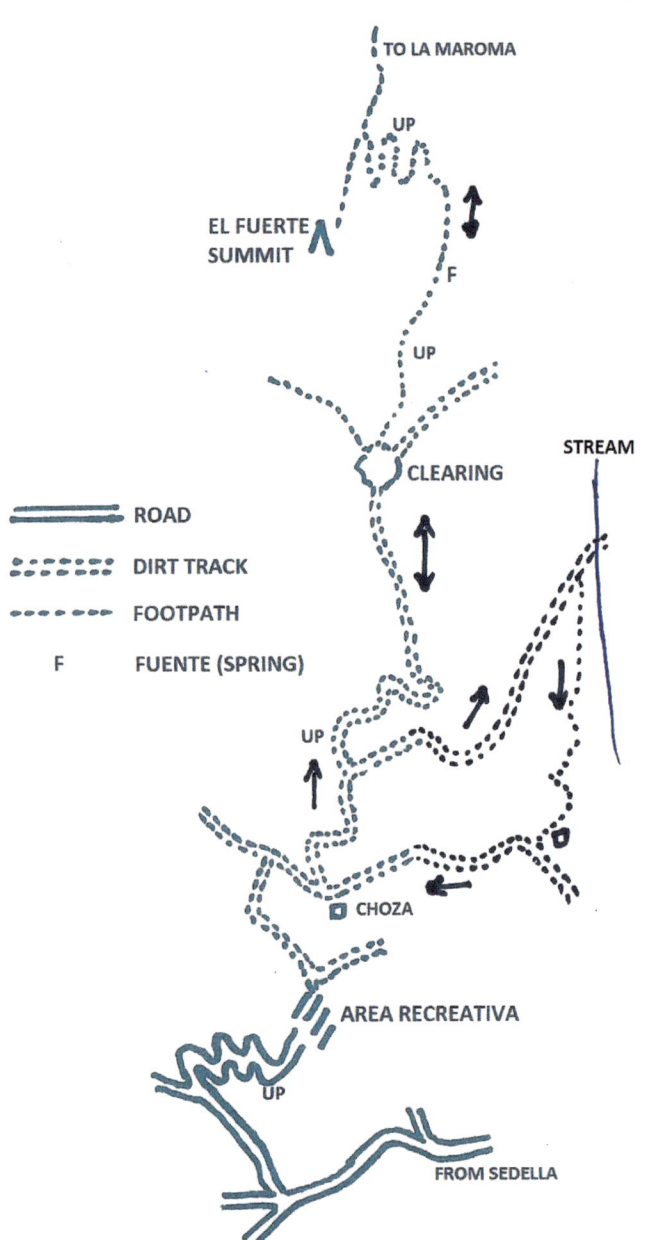

WALK NO. 6

SEDELLA TO THE SUMMIT OF EL FUERTE

El Fuerte is a subsidiary peak below the southern face of La Maroma. It is well worth its own walk. La Maroma is at 2,069 metres, and El Fuerte is over 500 metres short of that, but it is more easily accessible, has great views down to the sea, and is a good spot for inspecting the south face of La Maroma itself.

Distance	12 km
Ascent	700 metres
Overall grade	Moderate
Terrain	Tracks and footpaths
Exposure	None
Highest point	1,508 metres

Parts of this walk coincide with Walk 5, but with a different starting point and destination.

From Sedella, drive towards Canillas de Aceituno. On leaving Sedella, go round several sharp bends. Ignore a turn-off to the right signposted (at the time of writing) to *El Molino*. Continue round a few more bends and turn right on a track , opposite another turning to the left. (GPS reference here 407063 4080455). Drive up a narrow but well-surfaced road, round some very tight bends, ignoring any dirt roads and staying on tarmac. After five minutes you will reach a picnic site, where you should park. You will see an impressive statue of an ibex here. This is the start of the walk.

- From the picnic area, walk up the dirt track past the stone vulture. Ignore a track that goes to the right almost immediately, and go straight ahead, crossing a chain (which is to keep vehicles out). Go uphill on this broad track for about half a kilometre and at a junction turn right. After another half-kilometre you will reach La Choza del Guarda, a rebuilt shelter for forest workers. Keep to the left of the hut and above it, swinging to the left on the main track (not the lesser track, which starts at the *choza* itself).

- The track now zigzags uphill. At the next junction stay on the main track, which goes left. There is an old *era* (a threshing floor), which is now overgrown. Continue for a further 1.5 km approximately, until you reach a large clearing on the left. To the right is a slightly overgrown dirt road. Ignore it. Instead go left from the track into the clearing, and then immediately take a path uphill to the right (north). It is currently signposted as an ascent to La Maroma.

- El Fuerte is now directly above you. Ascend the footpath to the north, going up the right-hand (east) side of the hill. The path is stony at times, but well defined. It ascends steadily and passes a *fuente* (a spring) at one point. The views of La Maroma become more impressive as you near its southern slopes.

- The path swings left and goes into a series of zigzags, and then reaches a col (where the path for La Maroma levels out and goes to the right, but at the col El Fuerte is above on your left). Turn left at the col and follow a poorly defined path over rough but not too difficult ground to the summit. Once there you will find it is a fairly level area with good rocks on which to sit for a picnic, and with fine views in all directions. Historically there was a Roman fort on this summit but I can't find any trace of it, apart from bits of broken pottery on the ground – which could be Roman or Moorish, or indeed more recent.

- From the summit retrace your steps north to the col, and turn right down the footpath you ascended. Follow the zigzags, then go past the *fuente*, and continue until you reach the open clearing. Ignore a track going sharp

left from the clearing and take the main dirt track leading downhill to the south.
- When you reach the first junction take the track to the left, which is rarely used and slightly overgrown but easily passable. This track leads you generally downhill, to reach the stream called the Arroyo de la Fuente. However, just 50 metres or so before you reach the stream you will see a footpath going back to the right at a lower level, and starting next to a pine tree. This is the path to take. But, before you do so, you may like to take a break at the stream.
- From the stream return the 50 metres to the lower path, which starts with a little step down between pine trees, and follow this path. It goes on the level for a couple of kilometres, as the stream falls away below on the left. Eventually the path reaches a dirt road by some houses, which are in fact the waterworks for the village of Sedella. Turn left down the dirt track.
- As you enter this dirt road there is a large goat shed below on your right. Go past the goat shed. Ignore the first turn to the left and take the track swinging to the right, which leads you directly back to the picnic area where the walk began, passing by the Choza del Guarda on the way.

APPROXIMATE GPS REFERENCES (UTM)

Start	407051 4080944
Chozo del Guarda	407109 4081240
Left turn	407265 4081586
Clearing	407394 4082355
Summit	407370 4083054
Arroyo de la Fuente	407818 4082320

WALK NO. 7

WALK NO. 7 - SEDELLA TO LOS PICARICOS

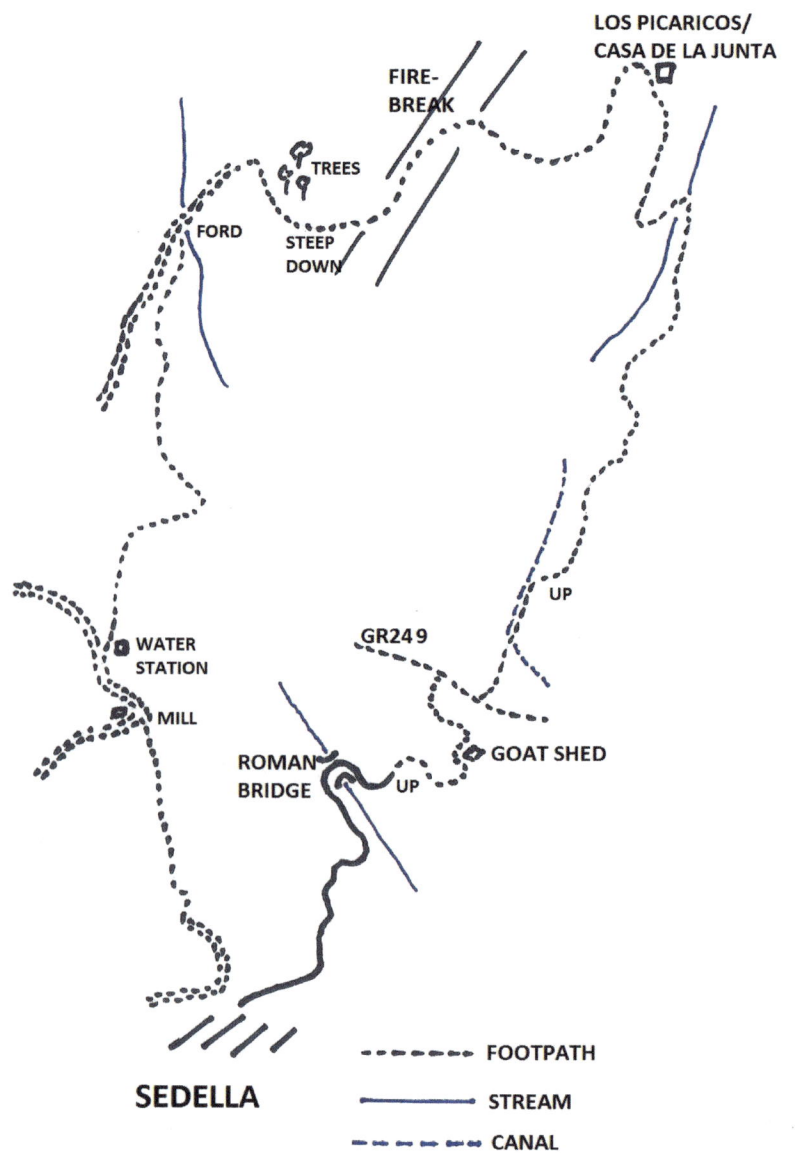

WALK NO. 7

SEDELLA TO LOS PICARICOS

A walk to a remote ruined inn below La Maroma. The walk follows some overgrown and scratchy paths but there is a reward for the effort, with two delightful stream valleys and an isolated, disused goat shed in a lovely valley.

Distance	11 km
Ascent	700 metres
Overall grade	Moderate to strenuous
Terrain	Tracks and footpaths (some overgrown)
Exposure	None
Highest point	1,263 metres

If it were ranked by distance and ascent this would class as a moderate walk, but the overgrown state of some of the paths and a descent down a steep, slippery slope make it fairly strenuous. Walking poles are a great advantage for the descent.

- From the bus stop, as you enter the western end of Sedella, walk along the street to pass some bars on the left. It is a maze of streets so I will not try to explain every step, but do not go downhill on any of the streets to the right. Keep going in a north-easterly direction. Look for a sign on Calle Granada pointing the way to the *Puente Romano* (the Roman Bridge) and Los Picaricos. Follow the arrow, passing the last houses in the village, one of which is called Casa de la Resculadera. At a fork by the house keep left and continue downhill, passing a mixture of modern villas and old goat sheds. After leaving the buildings behind the track swings right and then left as the Roman Bridge comes into view ahead (a good photo opportunity).

- Continue along the track and cross the bridge. Then go to the right uphill on a vague, stony path. It is marked occasionally by cairns, although it is indistinct at times. The path splits into two on more than one occasion, but the two branches usually return to join each other again. The only thing to watch is that you do not go along a path that runs parallel to the stream below. After five minutes' walk from the bridge you should be heading up and away from the stream. You will reach a large cairn. Then, as the ground starts to level out, you will see another large cairn on the left. At this point you will see the disused goat shed called La Herreriza above to your left.

- Make your way up to the goat shed and go around the back of it. Then go uphill to the right, on a vague path marked with one or two small cairns. You will enter a channel, which swings up to the left. Some way up here a small path goes up to the right, but a better path goes straight ahead. You can take either, but there are enough poor paths ahead of you on this walk, so this time take the better path straight ahead. It soon swings right and ascends a little to reach the long distance path GR 242/GR 249, marked with red and white paint on a signpost. Turn right along it to reach a junction with a sign on the left with an X. This means that this path up to the left is the wrong way – for the GR 249, but not for us. So turn left here, going past the sign with an X, and follow a footpath uphill.

- You will soon reach an *acequia*. Turn left and walk along the side of the canal, but watch out after only a short distance for a small bridge crossing the canal. Cross the canal and fork right here. The path is now sandy and stony, and is becoming considerably overgrown in places. However, it is not too difficult to follow at first. But, at GPS 408964 4081807, where it appears that the path goes straight on, make sure you swing to the right.

The correct path goes up to the right through some pine trees, and then swings left again at a slightly higher to level to go north. On a level stretch you will pass a path that goes off to the right, but ignore it. Continue along as the path starts to descend towards the valley below on your left. About 1.25 km from leaving the irrigation canal you will soon reach a beautiful little 'oasis' where the path crosses the stream called the Río de la Fuente – a lovely place for a rest on a sunny day.

- After you have crossed the stream you will see that the path swings to the left and then to the right uphill, to reach a junction of tracks where you should turn right, with the course of the stream now below on the right. You will soon go around a curve where suddenly the old goat house called Los Picaricos (shown on maps as Casa de la Junta) will come into view – a magnificent sight in a remote setting. Continue to the goat house. Just beyond and above the house take a path going back to the left (just west of south) and uphill.

- As you ascend gradually you will find a nice little group of rocks with a flat one on top. Continue on the path to reach a clearing, and go to the right to pick up the path again. It continues in a generally western direction to reach a broad firebreak. (*The views to your right of La Maroma are excellent here, and straight ahead as you reach the firebreak is El Fuerte. See Walk 6.*)

- Turn left to walk along the firebreak, and after about 250 metres take a very steep track down to the right (south-east, then east). Do not continue down the length of the firebreak itself. The track is very steep and the ground is loose, so it makes for a tricky fifteen minutes or so, and walking poles will come into their own. You will pass by a stand of pine trees, and shortly afterwards you will be relieved to turn right and follow the track down an easier slope to reach the river below (the Arroyo de la Fuente).

- Turn left, keeping to the left bank of the stream, and cross it at a ford. Turn left to go along the track, but after only a few metres take a left fork onto a narrower path, which starts with a step down between pine trees. This path goes along more or less on the level for about 1.5 km to reach a water pumping house. Go to the right to pick up another dirt track, and turn down to the left towards an old but renovated flour mill. But before you reach the mill you can take a left turn by a tree (GPS 407644 4080960) and then turn right alongside an *acequia*, to reach the far side of the water tank above the mill – a nice stretch of the walk.

- From the front of the mill take a track downhill and go straight ahead (south), to the right of a house with a fence. The track leads you down through olive and almond groves and then through irrigated terraces to reach the village of Sedella, where you began. When the track becomes concrete and swings left, go around the bend and take some steps down to the right to return to the street, at the end of which you will find the bus stop.

APPROXIMATE GPS REFERENCES (UTM)

Start	407677 4080158
Roman Bridge	408195 4080770
La Herreriza	408531 4080767
Río de la Fuente	409047 4081220
Los Picaricos	409071 4082693
Start of descent	408381 4082328
Arroyo de la Fuente	407796 4082224

CANILLAS DE ALBAIDA TO SEDELLA

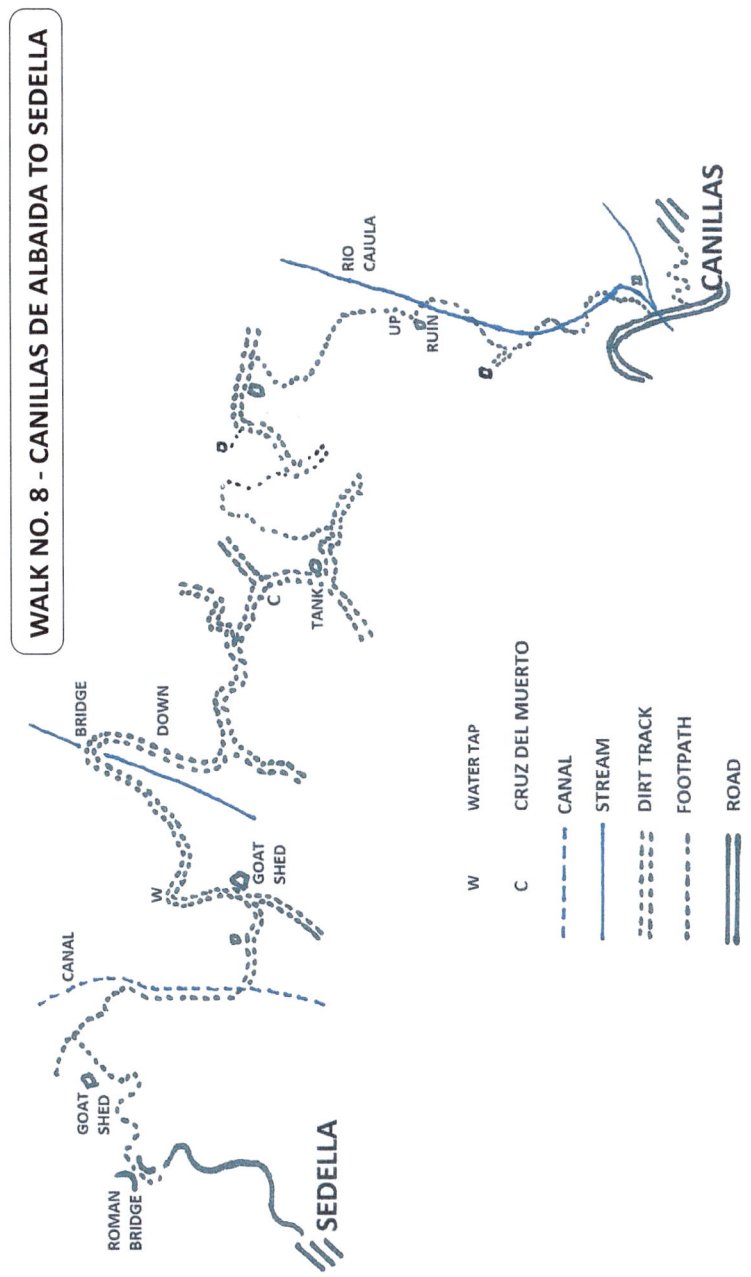

WALK NO. 8

CANILLAS DE ALBAIDA TO SEDELLA

A walk through the foothills of La Maroma from one ancient Moorish village to another.

Distance	13 km linear
Ascent	640 metres
Overall grade	Moderate
Terrain	Tracks and footpaths
Exposure	None
Highest point	864 metres

In the village of Canillas de Albaida, walk from Bar Cerezo to the far end of Calle Estación. Pass house no. 33. Where the street bends sharply uphill to the right go down some steps to the left, and then turn right downhill. Ignore a track to the left and keep on downhill, going round the right-hand side of a goat shed. This is an old Roman footpath, with a cobbled surface. Continue to the bottom of the hill.

- The path meets a road. Turn right along the road. Ignore a path that descends to the left to cross the Roman Bridge, and continue on the road. Cross a bridge over a stream and turn immediately right. Two streams meet here near a house. This route follows the stream coming in from the left, the Río Cájula. (You will cross the Río several times, on wooden bridges which at the time of writing are in generally good condition).

- Leaving the road, walk towards the house (a former flour mill) and go left to follow the stream, which will be on your right to begin with. You will walk through some orange and avocado groves. Cross the stream and walk on a level stretch, with the water to your left. Cross back again, and then the path ascends underneath limestone cliffs. Continue uphill and then on the level.

Soon you will cross the river twice more, and another uphill stretch through a fenced area leads to a clearing, from which a track goes uphill to a ruin ahead. Do not take this track but instead take the footpath to its right, signposted *Camino Río*.

- The path ascends just a little, and soon descends to reach the stream once more. Cross the stream again. On a level stretch ignore another path going up to the right, and then cross the stream for the last time, to ascend to a ruin. The path keeps to the right of the ruin and goes uphill again. It then levels out, crosses a minor watercourse, and finally ascends to reach a broad dirt track. Turn left along the dirt track.
- Within a few metres you will soon pass a ruin, which is used as stabling for horses (and dogs may bark here). The dirt track bends sharply to the left 200 metres further along. A very steep footpath goes straight ahead at this point, but do not take this path. Instead continue on the main track to the left, for a further 50 metres or so, and then ascend a path to the right, where the path has been reinforced with a stone wall.
- The path takes a zigzag route and can be somewhat difficult to follow. It can be hard to distinguish animal tracks from the footpath. So use your intuition to find the correct path, which goes steeply uphill. You will know that you are on the correct route when the path goes through a makeshift gate and leads you up between two wire fences.
- Soon the path levels out, and then continues sometimes level and sometimes uphill. You will join another path coming up from the right. Turn left along this path. Good views open up below. The path can be somewhat overgrown so take care with thistles and brambles, especially in the autumn, when dried-out thistles can be sharp. Continue to ascend through pinewoods and then out into the open again. The path swings to the left, levels out, and reaches a broad dirt track.

- Turn right along the track, which soon swings right and uphill, below a wooden lattice structure on the left. After about 200 metres, at a junction, the path continues slightly to the left and uphill, and very quickly reaches another dirt track on a level stretch. Turn right along it, and in less than five minutes you will reach a junction of dirt roads at the foot of a firebreak (this is La Cruz del Muerto, or the Dead Man's Cross).
- Turn left and follow this broad road downhill. Ignore a track going up sharply to the right, and later ignore another track going down to the left. The main track descends gradually, and then crosses a bridge over a stream among some eucalyptus trees. Keep on the track round more bends, to pass a water tank with a tap, and then round the next bend you will encounter a large goat shed below on your left. Leave the main track here and turn right to ascend another (minor) dirt track. It is quite steep at times.
- Keep right at a fork, and pass by a house. At the top of the rise go straight ahead. Ignore another minor track going to the right, and go a couple of paces further to meet an *acequia*.
- Turn right to follow the *acequia*, and walk on the concrete. It takes you up a slope, steeply at times, for about half a kilometre. When the canal levels out – just before it turns left and goes up steeply again – turn left on a path through some oleander bushes, to reach the crest of a small ridge. Continue on the other side of the ridge. You will see an old goat shed, La Herreriza, on the far side of the valley. That is your next target. There are paths all over the place, but the easiest way to get there is to keep to the path across the head of the valley, ignoring minor alternatives. At the far side of the valley continue uphill. At the top of the rise is a red and white marker, and then slightly beyond it is another marker post. Turn left here along a faint path, to descend through some rosemary bushes to the goat shed.

- At the goat shed go downhill to the left, across some ancient farm terraces, and look for a large cairn. Then take a footpath to the right just below the cairn. It descends in zigzags to the Roman Bridge of Sedella – a terrific photo opportunity. Cross the bridge, and follow the good track on the far side all the way into the village of Sedella.

APPROXIMATE GPS REFERENCES (UTM)

Start	411948 4078253
Camino Río	411610 4079159
La Cruz del Muerto	410506 4080091
Goat shed (fork right)	409201 4080203
La Herreriza	408518 4080727
Roman Bridge	408195 4080770

Roman bridge – **WALK 9**

WALK NO. 9

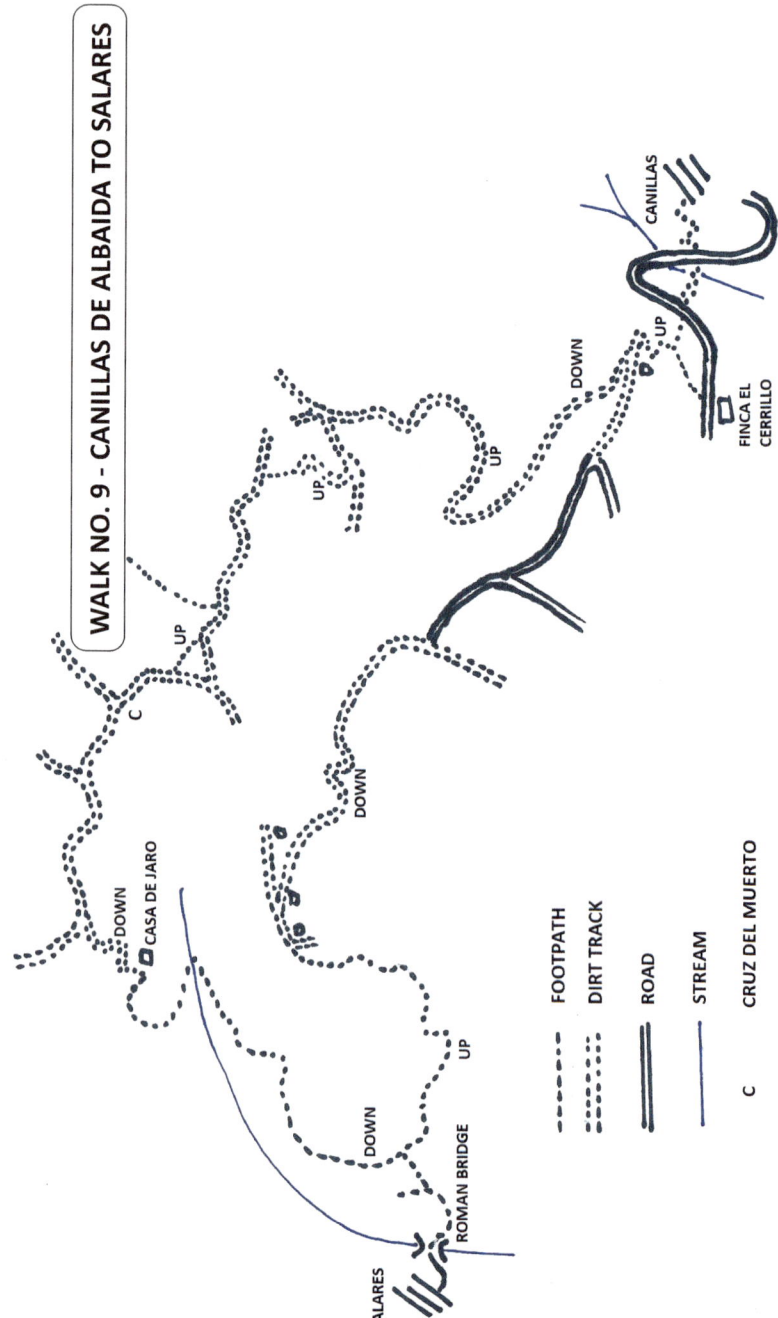

WALK NO. 9

CANILLAS DE ALBAIDA TO SALARES

A circular walk between two lovely old Moorish villages.

Distance	16 km (one way 10 km)
Ascent	800 metres (one way 530 metres)
Overall grade	Strenuous (one way moderate)
Terrain	Tracks and footpaths
Exposure	None
Highest point	875 metres

- In Canillas de Albaida walk from Bar Cerezo along Calle Estación to the far end, beyond house no. 33. When the street takes a sharp bend to the right go left down some steps, then go right. Ignore a track to the left and descend a stony mule track past a goat shed. Continue down the zigzags to reach a road. Turn right on the road for only a few metres, and almost immediately take a path down to the left, across the Roman Bridge. You will pass a sign saying *Calzada Romana* (Roman footpath). Follow the steep, zigzagging path up the other side to reach the road again.

- Cross the road. Then, just to your right, take a path going ahead into a valley. Follow the path zig-zag uphill to the right, to reach a house with a high wall. The house is in a semi-ruinous state at present (2022). Take the track around the right-hand side of the house, and then go left around the back of the house. Ignore a very minor track going to the right, and then almost immediately beyond it, at a major junction of tracks, take the track downhill to the right.

- This track is part concrete and part dirt track. It descends past a couple of houses and alongside olive and orange groves, then ascends and swings right. It is steep at times. Ignore any turn-offs. Stay on the main track. Pass a house on the left and continue ascending until, about 2 kilometres from the start of the track, there is a junction of tracks at the top of the hill. Take the first track left.

- As you ascend on a concreted section ignore a minor turn that goes sharply to the right, and then take a better track uphill to the right. It normally has a chain across the track to prevent vehicles passing. Zigzag uphill steeply to reach a clearing. At the far right-hand corner of the clearing, between the last olive tree and the first pine tree, go two or three metres uphill and take a path that runs on the level, keeping to the right of a vine field and to the left of the pinewoods. The path soon reaches a dirt track. Take this track to the left.

- Continue on the track through the pine trees until it swings to the right to climb steeply, with a wooden trellis above on the left. At the top of the rise, at a minor junction, a footpath goes uphill and ahead and soon reaches another dirt track. Turn right along the track to reach La Cruz del Muerto (the Dead Man's Crossroads), which is a broad T-junction at the foot of a firebreak. At the junction turn left on a dirt road, which goes gradually downhill. Ignore another track going up sharply to the right. The village of Salares will come into view below on the left.

- When you are 1 kilometre from La Cruz del Muerto turn left on to a broad, zigzagging track. Go downhill to pass a water tank and a helicopter pad (for fire control). After passing to the left of a fence, and then swinging to the right, you will soon reach a ruined farm, the Casa de Haro, with a *fuente* (a water tap) below to the right. Go down past the *fuente*, and then follow a path down to

- the left. There are animal tracks here, which make the main path difficult to follow, but there are waymarks to show the line of the path.
- The path descends and then swings left. When you reach a valley you will see that the path leads over a few rocks and turns right to cross a watercourse (which is usually dry), and then turns right again on the far side of the valley. Follow the left side of the valley, passing above some poplars and through holm oak trees. At one point, where the path appears to go straight ahead, and where an arrow points back the way you came, the path actually goes down to the right, steeply past some trees, and then continues along the side of the valley. It can be a bit confusing along here. At GPS (approximately) 409310 4079643, what looks like a path straight ahead leads you into undergrowth.
- Keep to the path as Salares comes into view ahead on the right. The path ascends slightly and then swings downhill to the right, to where another path comes in from the left. (Make a note of this point for the return leg of the walk.) Turn right here.
- Continue downhill until you join another, stony path, on which you should turn right downhill to cross the Roman/Arab Bridge of Salares (a great photo opportunity) and go on into the village, passing below the church tower, which was originally a minaret. The semi-ruinous walls here are a mixture of Roman, Moorish and Spanish architecture. You may find the old churchyard interesting.
- If you have opted for the one-way route, this is the end of the walk. But if you are doing the full circuit read on.
- For the return route go back to cross the Roman Bridge. At the far side of the bridge the track goes left, past a water tap. Then, by a fence, a path goes uphill to the right. Follow this stony path uphill. At a junction of

paths take the left fork. And then, by a post with an arrow, ignore a minor path to the left. You will now be on the same path you descended earlier and will continue on it until the next junction.

- On a fairly steep ascent you will soon reach the junction that you ought to be able to recognise from the outward leg. Ignore the arrow that points left and go straight ahead, steeply uphill. (A cross indicates that this is the wrong way. But for this walk it is the right way.) This path continues relentlessly up the hillside. Near some rocks take a rest for a good view of Salares, Sedella and La Maroma. This is a steep and continual ascent.

- Continue until the path levels off at a junction of broader tracks. Go ahead, keeping to the left-hand track. Pass some houses on the right and then take the first track to the right. Follow this good track, passing some farmhouses and a few modern villas, until you reach a junction with wire fencing surrounding a farm. (There is a signpost here, pointing back to Fogarate.) At this point take the concrete track downhill to the left to pass between two raisin farms, and continue down as the track becomes a surfaced minor road.

- At a fork go left and walk downhill. Where the road swings to the right continue straight ahead on a track with houses on your right. Go downhill to another junction and once more go straight on, with some houses on your right. You will soon reach a semi-ruined house, which you passed early in the walk. Go just beyond the house and turn right, then go downhill on a footpath to meet a road. Cross the road and descend to cross the Roman Bridge.

- Go to the right on the road for just a few metres and then take the mule track uphill to the left to return to Canillas.

CANILLAS DE ALBAIDA TO SALARES

APPROXIMATE GPS REFERENCES (UTM)

Start	411948 4078253
Calzada Romana	411669 4078418
Left turn on to track	411412 4079484
Left turn on to track	411165 4079649
La Cruz del Muerto	410506 4080091
Casa de Jaro	409632 4080145
Cross stream bed	409641 4079908
Path down	409394 4079728
Junction of paths	408973 4079210
Top of hill	409695 4079589

Casa de Haro – **WALK 9**

WALK NO. 10

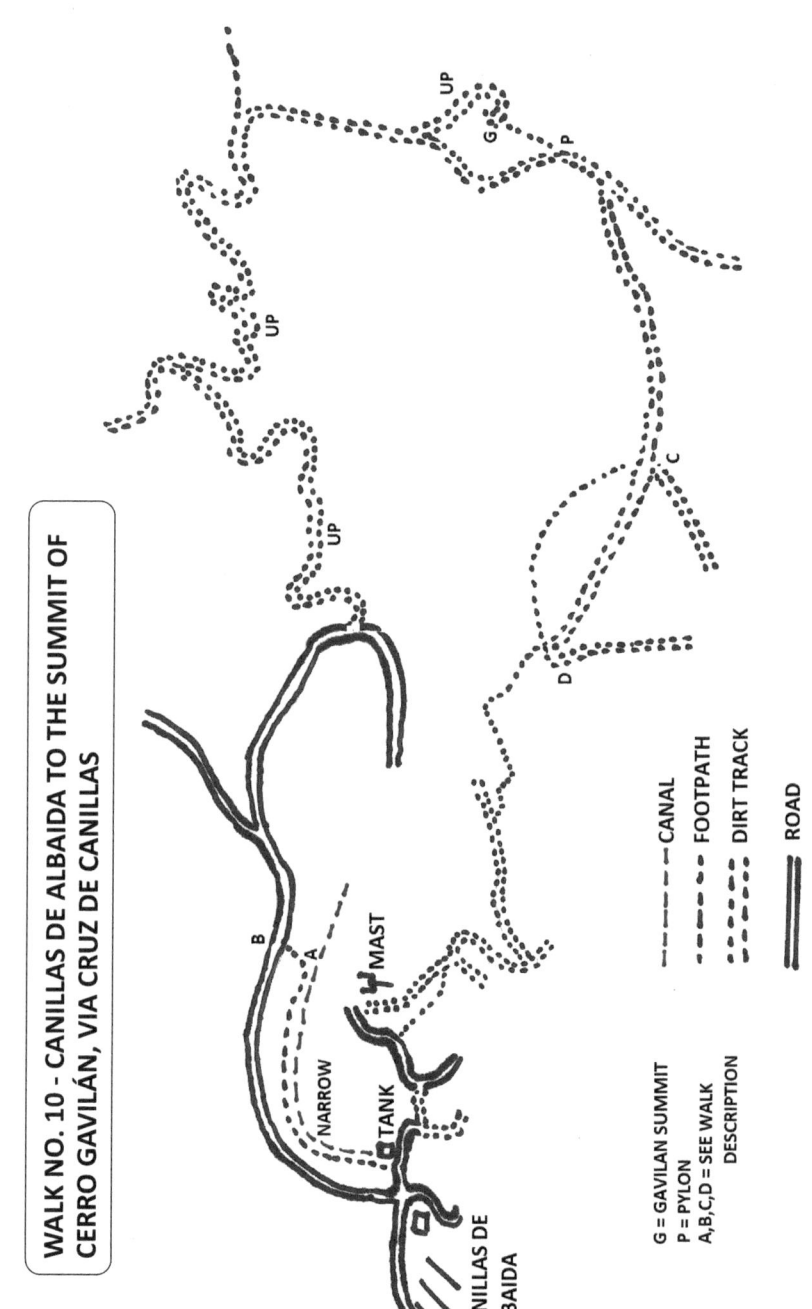

WALK NO. 10

CANILLAS DE ALBAIDA TO THE SUMMIT OF CERRO GAVILÁN, VIA CRUZ DE CANILLAS

An ascent from the village to a fire control lookout, with great views of the sierra.

Distance	12 km
Ascent	650 metres
Overall grade	Moderate
Terrain	Tracks and footpaths
Exposure	One narrow path, but it is avoidable
Highest point	1,136 metres

This walk contains optional moderate or strenuous sections at two points in the walk. The final descent is on steep and stony ground.

- From the Canillas de Albaida cemetery walk uphill on the perimeter road of the village, high above the valley below. At the top of the hill, passing the Santa Ana chapel, pass a new house on the left, and you will reach a junction of minor roads.

- For the easier option here, turn left on the road towards La Fábrica de la Luz (there is hardly any traffic and the views are nice) to reach Point B on the sketch map.

- For the harder option – which needs a reasonable head for heights – ignore the left turn at the junction that is signposted to La Fábrica and instead go straight ahead and slightly uphill. You will very soon reach a fenced-off reservoir, which feeds the local irrigation system. Turn left immediately before the fence and take a path alongside an irrigation canal. The path is narrow and airy, and sometimes has a drop to the left, so take care. At times you will need to walk on the concrete edge of the canal. This will not suit anybody with vertigo, but you can avoid it by taking the road route described above. After just less than 1 kilometre on this path, and at Point A on the sketch map, turn left down a track to reach the road below at Point B.

- From Point B continue down the road. At a junction near a signpost for the Parque Natural take the right fork. The road passes below a house on the right, and then ascends gradually. Stay on the surfaced road as it continues easily upwards, until it widens and bends very sharply to the right (this is a turning place for quarry trucks). At this bend do not follow the road, but keep straight ahead on a dirt track.

- The track ascends gradually in zigzags, with views to the west improving all the time. You will soon be able to see the coast over your left shoulder. Continue until, after about 2.5 kilometres on the dirt road, you arrive at a junction, where the main track goes sharp left and another dirt road goes uphill to the right. Ascend this dirt road to the right. It has some concreted sections, but remains a track rather than a road. It continues to climb towards the rocky peak of Cerro Atalaya, passing through some pleasant pinewoods before emerging into the open.

- Continue up the bendy track and ignore any turn-offs, until you reach a white sandy area where the track levels off and swings very sharply to the right. Ignore a good path that goes to the left on the apex of the bend. (It is the Silk Route. See Walk 17.) Instead follow the main track round to the right.

- At the next junction of tracks take the concrete track uphill to the left. It soon leads you to the fire watch lookout station at the summit of Cerro Gavilán. At the summit you may not enter the official building, but you can ascend the rocky hilltop to the side of it, and the

CANILLAS DE ALBAIDA TO THE SUMMIT OF CERRO GAVILÁN

views are brilliant in all directions (which explains why they put a fire watch station here, of course.)

- From the summit, return along the same track you ascended. Go round the first bend to the left, and then look for a path going downhill steeply to the right. Take this path down, through some rocky areas, to reach the main track again near some pine trees and a pylon. At this point you will rejoin the dirt track you were following earlier.

- Continuing ahead you will see that the main track splits in two. The left branch leads towards Cómpeta. For Canillas de Albaida take the right-hand (lower) fork. Follow this easy track along until you reach another fork, with a large cairn, where a path goes down to the left. Keep to the right instead. This is Point C on the sketch map.

- *For the harder option here, turn right at Point C*. Do not take a track that goes to a pylon. Instead keep to the right of the pylon and ascend over rough ground to the summit of a hill, which is generally not named on maps, although it is sometimes known as the Mosquin. There is a cairn at the very top, and there are great views to Canillas below. Continue over the top of the hill and keep going in the same direction with no path, descending steeply over stony and scrubby ground. At the foot of the hill you will meet a dirt track, at Point D.

- *For the easier option at Point C*, take the right fork, but do not take the minor track to the pylon, and do not ascend the hill to the right. Stay on the main track, with the hill above on your right, to reach Point D.

- At Point D the main track doubles sharply back to the left. But instead take a path straight ahead (north), following the crest of a broad ridge. After a couple of hundred metres the path starts to descend the hill to the left. Follow the path down. Near some cairns another path goes very, very steeply down to the right towards a radio mast. Ignore it and stay on the ridge, descending to the west, on a steep and stony path. Pass a lone pine tree, and shortly afterwards you will reach a stand of pine trees, where a path goes downhill to the right to reach a broader track by a cairn (put there originally by me).

- Take this track downhill to the left. It becomes gradually easier, and reaches a much wider dirt road, where you should turn right. Ignore another track going off to the left, and shortly afterwards take a footpath below on the left, marked by a cairn. The path goes on the level for a while. At a junction of paths keep left. This path leads to a small telephone antenna (not the big mast above) and then goes down to the left to join a road, which descends steeply towards Canillas. Go down the road, but just round the first bend look for a footpath on the right that leads down past the disused sporting installations and back to the village.

APPROXIMATE GPS REFERENCES (UTM)

Start	411848 4078357
Reservoir	412301 4078395
Point A	412868 4078638
Point B	412955 4078653
Dirt road starts	413694 4078581
Go right	414563 4078950
Swing right	415232 4078648
Summit	415130 4078082
Pylon	414979 4077791
Point C	414226 4077648
Point D	413677 4078000
Path down	413553 4078140

CASA DE LA MINA CIRCUIT

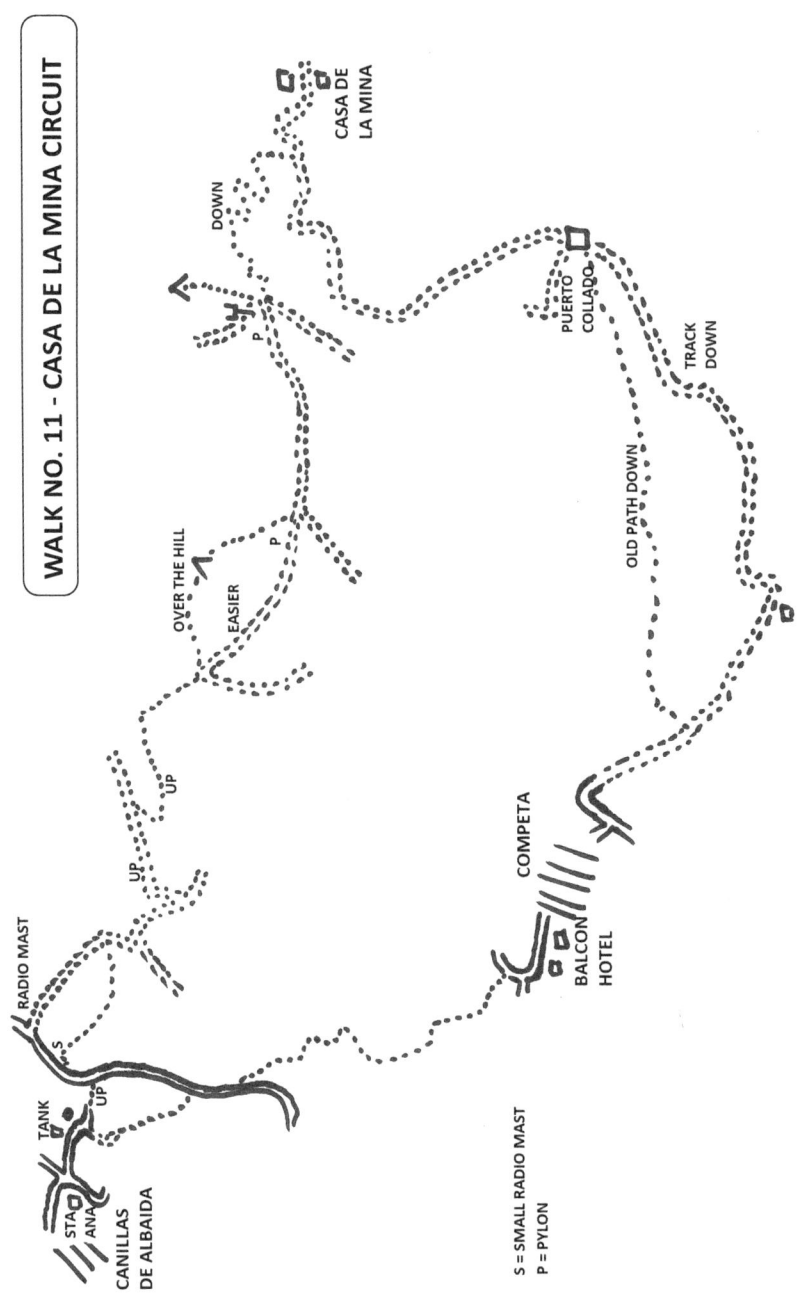

WALK NO. 11

CASA DE LA MINA CIRCUIT

A circular walk from Canillas de Albaida, via the base of Cerro Gavilán, to the remote hotel of Casa de la Mina, returning via Puerto Collado and Cómpeta.

Since it is a circular route you can start and finish the walk in either Cómpeta or Canillas.

Distance	15 km
Ascent	710 metres
Overall grade	Moderate
Terrain	Tracks and footpaths
Exposure	None
Highest point	1,050 metres

- Walk up to the Santa Ana chapel at the top of the village in Canillas de Albaida. Go forward to a road junction (with the door of the chapel behind you). Ignore the left fork and go straight ahead uphill, passing an irrigation reservoir on the left. Beyond it, at a white water tank, do not take the lower – immediate – right turn, but instead take the higher road, going uphill to the right of the tank and passing a motor-home park on the left and a house on the right. Take a short footpath uphill straight ahead to reach a road.

- Turn left and walk up the road, around a steep right-hand bend. Just before the next left-hand bend take a rough stony footpath on the right, ascending past a small transmitter mast (not the large mast at the top of the hill). The footpath goes to the right. At a junction of paths keep right. When you reach a dirt road go to the right along it. Ignore another track to the right, and continue slightly uphill. You will very soon reach a

- large pine tree on the right, with a pile of stones and a great view back to the village. At this point a track goes uphill to the left. Take this track.

- The stony and sandy track ascends steadily. After half a kilometre look for a cairn marking the start of a footpath going uphill to the right. (There may be more than one cairn. The correct one is directly below a stand of pine trees above to the right.) The path ascends to the pine trees and then turns left, to follow the crest of a broad ridge. Follow the path uphill, quite steeply at times, as it ascends in more or less a straight line to reach the top of the ridge. *(I created this path myself over twenty years ago.)*

- Near the top of the ridge the path swings to the right. At the top you will have great views to the Sierra Almijara and the peak of El Lucero. Continue along the ridge to the right to reach a sharp bend in a dirt road. Take the left branch of the dirt track, which ascends easily, and which soon meets another track coming up from Cómpeta.

- Turn left along this track. Follow it gently uphill, and then on a level stretch, to reach a junction at the foot of the hill of Cerro Gavilán. There is a pylon at the junction. You can see the Hotel Casa de la Mina below. To the right of the pylon a cairn marks the start of a path downhill. Take this path, which will lead you down to reach a dirt road at a point 100 metres from the hotel. Turn left on the dirt road to reach the hotel.

- On the right of the road is the old hostal, Casa de la Mina. On the left is the modern hotel with the same name. You may or may not find either of these open for a coffee, a beer or a snack. They open and close irregularly, so don't rely on refreshments. But the gardens of the hostal make a good place for a rest, and the views to the coast are good.

- Retrace your steps for 100 metres from Casa de la Mina and then continue on the broad track past the end of the path you just descended. Continue to walk up the wide dirt road for 1.5 kilometres until you reach a viewpoint with a fence at a junction of tracks. This is Puerto Collado. You can see Nerja on the coast, and the whole of the Sierra Almijara inland.

- At Puerto Collado a track goes uphill to the right, and another goes downhill to the left. There was a good path in between them, going down the valley from here, but it was destroyed by a forest fire in 2014, so you have a choice to make. You can descend the valley over rough ground, or you can walk down the dirt road on the left. The condition of the route down the valley is uncertain, since the land is still recovering (in early 2018) from the major wildfire. If you opt for the dirt road, follow it round some bends. The road is broad and dusty, but the views are great. You will pass a lonely house on a bend, and at the bottom of the hill you will encounter the bottom of the valley referred to above.

- From here stay on the track. Soon you will pass some houses on the right, at the Urbanización Cruz del Monte. The road becomes surfaced and then swings to the left at a junction. Turn right at a small shrine to reach the town of Cómpeta.

- As you wander through the labyrinth of streets in Cómpeta look for the church tower in order to find the plaza in the town centre. Cross the plaza with your back to the church and take the street going to the left above a balustrade at the top side of the square. This will lead you to the Hotel Balcon. Go past the hotel. When the road swings right follow it part of the way around the bend, and then take a wide path on the left between a fence and a wall. Follow this path through some olive groves and irrigated farm terraces until it reaches a road.

CASA DE LA MINA CIRCUIT

- Turn right along the road for 300 metres, where a cairn on the left marks the start of a path back to Canillas de Albaida.

APPROXIMATE GPS REFERENCES (UTM)

Start	412041 4078196
Left turn	412860 4077988
Footpath	413319 4078123
Pylon and cairn	414989 4077803
Casa de la Mina	415481 4077668
Puerto Collado	415009 4076612
Valley bottom	414376 4076505
Footpath	412722 4077080

Descent from El Lucero – **WALKS 15 & 16**

WALK NO. 12

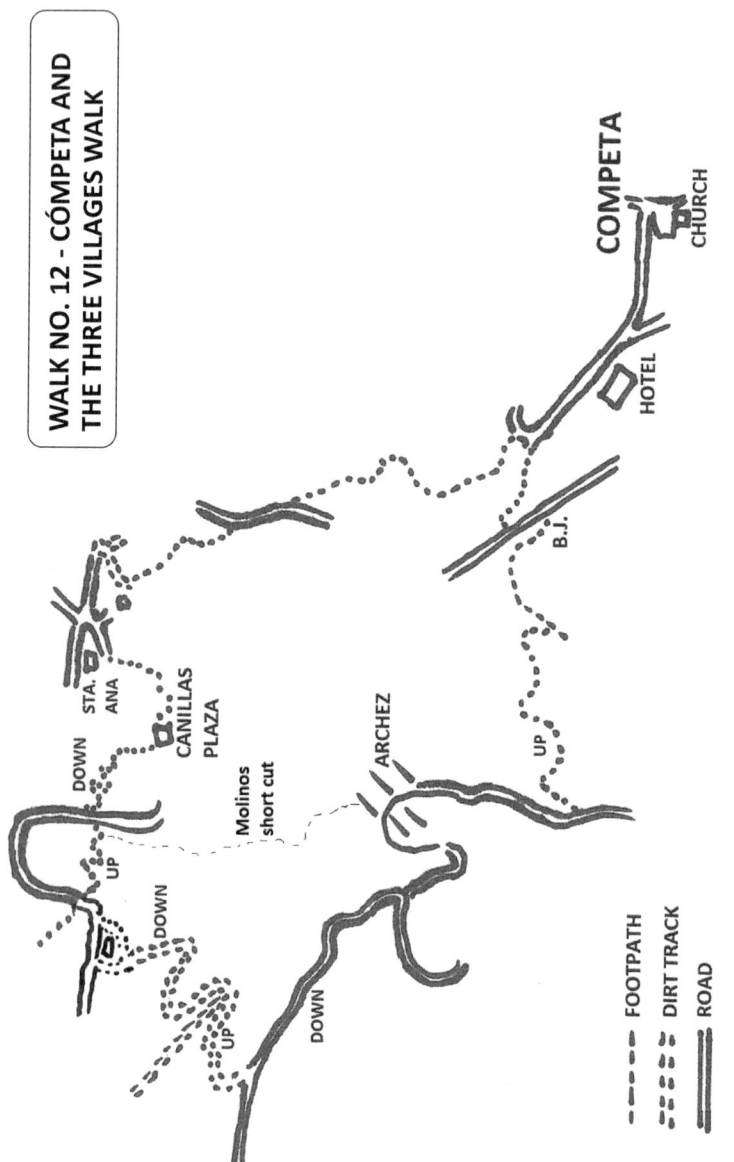

WALK NO. 12

CÓMPETA AND THE THREE VILLAGES WALK

A walk connecting the three main villages of the Cómpeta area along a mix of mule tracks, footpaths and just a little bit of road walking.

Distance	12 km
Ascent	650 metres
Overall grade	Moderate
Terrain	Tracks, roads and footpaths
Exposure	None
Highest point	666 metres

- Note: the walk can be shortened by following the "Ruta de los Molinos" from Canillas to Archez, as described below.

- Go to the highest part of the main square of Cómpeta and turn left on the street that goes behind the balustrade. Follow the street round a bend and continue to the very end of the street, where it joins a road near the Hotel Balcon. Walk past the hotel and you will find the chapel of San Anton on the left. Beyond the chapel a path goes straight ahead downhill. But, instead of descending that path, turn right up the road for 20 metres and turn left on to a broad track by a fence. As it passes some irrigated terraces and olive groves the track soon becomes a footpath and goes alongside the main irrigation canal (now buried). You will see all the local produce such as onions, potatoes, lettuces, beans, marrows and corn, as well as avocado and olive trees. Look out for the agave succulents, which grow for several years then flower and die.

- Turn right when the path reaches a road and continue on the road for 300 metres. Then look for a cairn on the left and take a footpath there. It continues through terraced farmland and leads to the top of the village of Canillas de Albaida. Above some houses the path turns into a broader track. Follow the track round to the right, and near a white water tank go left. Descend to the chapel of Santa Ana, which has great views into the natural park.

- Ascend to the chapel to look at the view. Then, to the left side of the building, take some steps down into a car park and turn left. Take the first street to the right and go downhill. Turn left to enter the labyrinth of streets in the older part of town and look for the main square of the village, where you will find the town hall, the church, Hotel Posada la Plaza, and its bar/restaurant.

- From the door of the restaurant, go left and walk past the right-hand side of the church. Then, in a small square, go diagonally left downhill and pass by a corner full of trees and flowers. Go straight across the next street and down a few steps. Then go to the right and walk downhill on a stony goat track to pass a goat shed, and keep on walking down to a road. Turn right on the road for a few metres, then go left on a footpath to reach the Roman Bridge (**).

- ** As you cross the Roman Bridge you can take a short cut to Archez, by following a path to the left, signposted *Ruta de los Molinos*. The path follows the right bank of the stream. Stay on this side of the stream, following green and white markers, as the path goes past some old ruined mills.

- If you do not opt for the short cut, cross the Roman Bridge, and ascend the zigzag path on the far side.

- When the path reaches a road turn left along it, steeply uphill and around a right-hand bend. Then turn left on a track signposted *Lisa Katrina*. Keep right at a fork and pass below the gardens of Finca el Cerrillo, a delightful hotel. Turn left beyond the *finca* on the next dirt/concrete track downhill. Pass some houses, and turn right at a junction. Keep left at the next junction, follow the track into a valley, and then stay on the dirt track as it ascends quite steeply and then turns left. Continue until you reach the main **Á**rchez to Salares road. There is very little traffic on the road here, but take care. Turn left and walk down the road for half a kilometre until you reach a right-hand bend, where there is a bench with a lovely view down on to the village of **Á**rchez.

- (Note the view of the church tower below. It is a sixteenth-century church with an older tower, which was originally a minaret. It is one of four almost identical towers. The others are in nearby Salares, and in not-so-nearby Tunis and Tremec**é**n in North Africa.)

- Continue down the main road beyond the bench for just a few metres more and turn left to descend a paved street into **Á**rchez village centre. On the way you will pass some farm buildings and a chicken coop, and also some groves of avocado and nispero trees. Cross the river over a bridge and turn left alongside the river. The road swings to the right and leads to a junction where you can turn right, uphill, to reach the church and its minaret/bell tower. In the street to the side of the tower there are some ceramic plaques showing the local produce, and how the tower was built (in Spanish, of course).

- Go round (anti-clockwise) behind the church, turn left to pass the main door, and then turn right to reach a car park with a very nice bar. Continue out of the far end of the car park, pass a traffic light (the only one in the area), and go on to join a road. Do not turn right over the bridge but go straight on along the road, away from the village. Pass some industrial buildings and then go round a couple of bends to reach a point where a signpost on the left indicates a footpath. Turn left on this path. Then take a path to the right that ascends to reach a house higher up on the right.

- Go past the house and ascend the path to reach an area that has been recently (2017) planted with trees. Turn right, steeply uphill here, and you will see that the footpath continues up and to the left. It becomes a broader dirt track. Follow it up until it reaches another dirt track, near a house with a gate, where you should turn left. Continue on this track until it reaches the main Canillas to Cómpeta road near the Jarel bodega. Turn left on the road. After just a few metres turn right, where a path goes up to the right, and then go up some steps past an irrigation tank. Joining another path turn right, pass a stable, and you will soon reach the edge of Cómpeta at the chapel of San Anton.

APPROXIMATE GPS REFERENCES (UTM)

Start	413084 4076765
Start of path	412722 4077080
End of path	412561 4077714
Goat track down	411823 4078292
Track	411421 4078339
Road	410979 4077888
Path up	411661 4076990

Cerro Atalaya – **WALK 13**

LA FÁBRICA DE LA LUZ TO CERRO VERDE AND CERRO ATALAYA

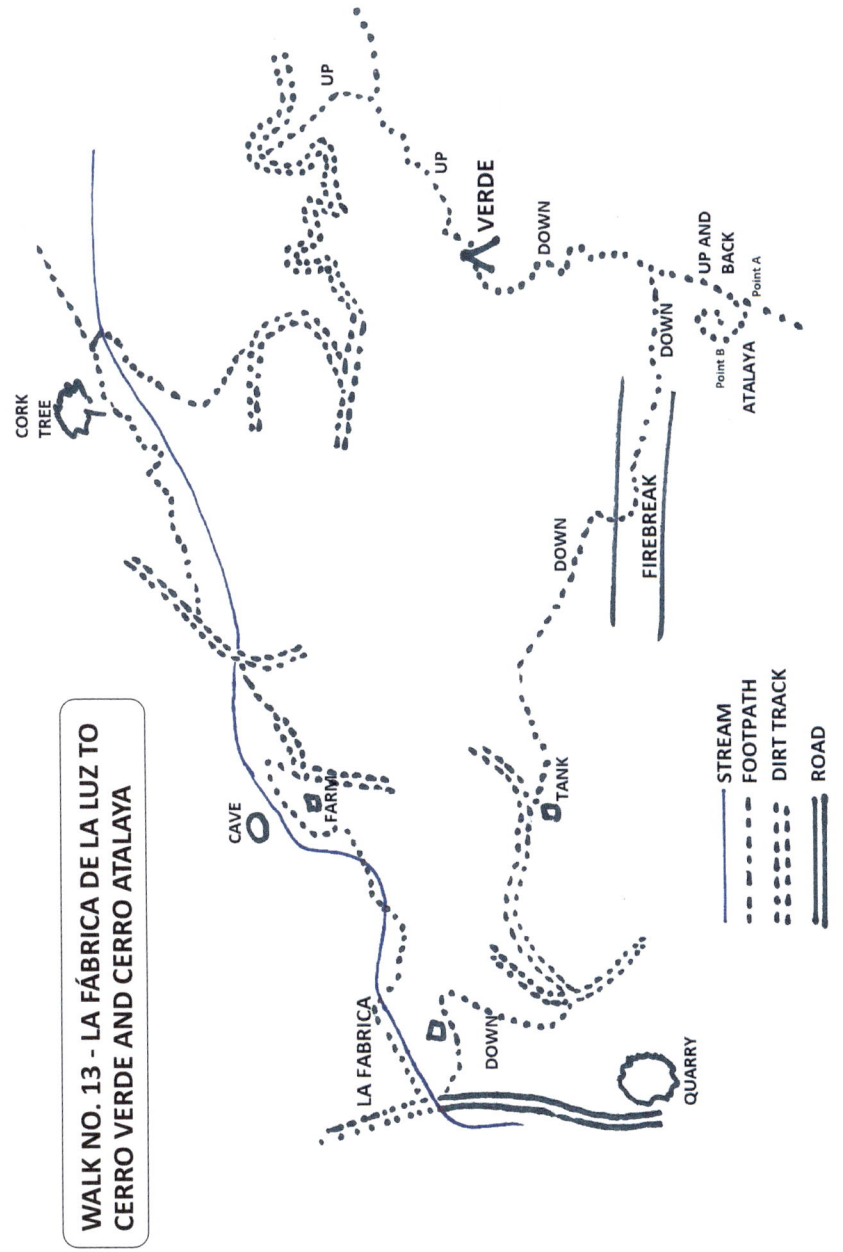

WALK NO. 13

LA FÁBRICA DE LA LUZ TO CERRO VERDE AND CERRO ATALAYA

A circular walk from a local beauty spot to the summits of two of the area's intermediate peaks. The second peak involves an easy scramble, but requires a head for heights. It is optional, and can be avoided. But a short, airy passage early in the walk cannot be avoided.

Distance	13 km
Ascent	800 metres
Overall grade	Moderate to strenuous
Terrain	Tracks, roads and footpaths
Exposure	A very short high and narrow path
Highest point	1,332 metres

The walk begins at La Fábrica de la Luz, near Canillas de Albaida. La Fábrica was formerly a water-powered electricity generating station, and there are still remnants of the waterworks. Nowadays it is a delightful picnic area, alongside a stream which runs all year round.

- Drive from the Santa Ana chapel at the top of Canillas de Albaida, following a signpost saying *La Fábrica, Area Recreativa*. Take the left turn at a fork. Then ignore another left turn and continue on to pass a limestone quarry. Park at the very end of the asphalt road, where there is a car park with barbecue facilities and tables.

- From the car park walk straight ahead to the stream and cross it, wherever you find easiest. Take the path to the right on the opposite bank of the stream. You will soon cross it three times more, as you pass through an area of (poisonous) oleander bushes. There are crude stepping stones on some of the crossings but if the water is high it can be difficult to get across with dry feet. After the fourth crossing, when you are to the right of the stream, the path goes slightly uphill to pass through a terraced walnut farm at Cortijo del Chato, with the Honeymaker's Cave coming into view on the left.

- The cave was used as a goat shed until Pepe the goatherd retired in 2015. The walnuts are still farmed by his family. Stay on the path and pass below the farmhouse, where Pepe's dogs may bark at you but should not cause you any problem. The path goes past the house, and then swings sharply right to reach a dirt track by a gate. Do not enter the farmyard. Instead turn left along the track. Keep straight on when you meet another track coming down from the right. The track descends slightly, and beyond a tree it becomes a path.

- The path soon crosses the watercourse again, although at this point it is often dry. The path meets a dirt/concrete track. Do not turn right on this track, but go ahead on it. It will take you gradually uphill on the north side of the valley. Follow the track uphill, but keep a keen eye open for a footpath to the right with a cairn and an arrow pointing the way. (If you reach a building you have gone too far.) Go to the right on this path, and keep going until you reach a large cork tree. The low wall and the wire fence by the cork tree mark the boundary of the chestnut farm of El Chaparral. You can now see another cave on the opposite side of the valley. This route will take you above it, although the path is invisible from here.

- From the cork tree stay on the footpath. After just a few minutes, at the bottom of a short descent, leave the main path and turn sharp right by some rocks to cross the stream (which is usually dry). This right turn is not entirely obvious, so ideally you should use the GPS reference given below. If you reach a ruined house above on the left you have gone too far.

- Once you are across the watercourse look for a narrow path going steeply up to the right, after bashing through undergrowth for a few metres. Then the gradient eases. The path will take you along the hillside and uphill. You will soon reach a rocky outcrop, which requires an easy scramble to get over. (Those with severe vertigo may have a problem here, but it is only a short stretch.)

- The path now goes below a rocky overhang and continues over a very short, narrow stretch to another short and easy scramble, where the descent on the far side may cause problems for vertigo sufferers. (*Take care here. For experienced hill walkers this is easy, but it may be daunting for those without the experience.*) Once you are across the scramble the path improves. Go along it as it swings to the left into a valley. The path now ascends and joins another dirt/concrete track. Continue up the track until it levels out. Cross a dry watercourse below a wall and follow the track, which is sometimes sandy, as it bends to the right to reach a major dirt road.

- Go left on the major dirt road for about twenty minutes. There are many bends in the road and the next path may be a little difficult to find, although it is marked with cairns. At a point where the track is going in a virtually northerly direction there is a rocky peak ahead of you. The dirt track swings sharply right, and on the right of the track there is a loose, sandy patch of ground. The GPS reference is 416200 4080606. Go up this sandy hillside on the right, and then go through some patchy rosemary and gorse. After 25 metres or so you will find a good path, which ascends the hillside towards the col below the peak of Cerro Verde, which you can now see ahead to your right.

- Follow the path up towards the south-east until it reaches the top of a ridge, at a T-junction of paths. Views to the coast and the high peaks open up here.

Turn right on a good path, and follow it all the way to the top of Cerro Verde. There are some rocky patches to cross, but there is no technical difficulty. The summit (1,332 metres) is marked by a trig point to the left of a stand of pine trees. The view includes Cerro Atalaya (our next port of call on this walk), the coast, and whole of the Sierra Almijara. There are excellent picnic spots for cooler weather on the rocks to the left before the trees, and in hotter weather on rocks among the trees.

- From the trig point go back to the path that you ascended and turn left along it. Swing left beyond the trees. Follow the path, which descends – steeply at times – to reach a col below Cerro Atalaya. Here a path goes downhill to the right. Ignore it for now and go straight ahead and uphill, with the rocky face of Cerro Atalaya above on the right. The path skirts the eastern side of the peak. After about 250 metres uphill walking from the col, and where the path starts to go downhill (Point A on the sketch map), turn sharply back to the right to follow a faint path up towards the rocks. (*From this point on there is a little exposure. If you do not want to ascend Cerro Atalaya then wait here for the rest of your group to return.*)

- Cross a few rocks and look for a faint path going left across loose ground, with the peak still above on your right. Do not try to ascend directly. It is dangerous. Go horizontally along below the peak, and after a couple of zigzags on the vague path look for a natural gap in the rocks above you and go through it (Point B). Leave your walking poles here for collection on the way down. Once you are through the gap swing to the right, ascend over some rocks and then scramble up to the left, squeezing between a tree and a rock face. It is an easy, short – but exposed – scramble to the top. The view from the bare rock summit is stunning.

- Taking care, scramble down by the route of ascent. Pass through the gap in the rocks (Point B) once more, and return the way you came. Reaching the path at Point A go left and down to the col once more.

- At the col turn left downhill. The path descends through pine trees, and then goes along a bare and stony firebreak. After 200 metres or so keep over towards the right-hand edge of the firebreak. Then look for a cairn that marks a path downhill to the right into a pine forest. Make sure you find this path, which swings to the right and then goes steeply down, to reach a dirt track near a water tank after ten or fifteen minutes. (Note the enormous tadpoles in the tank.)
- Turn left on the track, with the Honeymaker's Cave soon in sight in the valley below, and continue to where another track comes in from the right. Just beyond this track two cairns mark a footpath that takes you downhill to return to La Fábrica de la Luz, where the walk began.

APPROXIMATE GPS REFERENCES (UTM)

Start	413518 4080210
Left on the track	414614 4080646
Cork tree	415590 4081129
Cross stream	415676 4081144
Scrambles	415551 4080987
Join dirt road	415594 4080501
Footpath	416200 4080606
Cerro Verde	415847 4079991
Col	415812 4079522
Way up	415697 4079321
Cerro Atalaya	415710 4079401
Water tank	414767 4079934

WALK NO. 14 - MALAS CAMAS FROM LA FÁBRICA

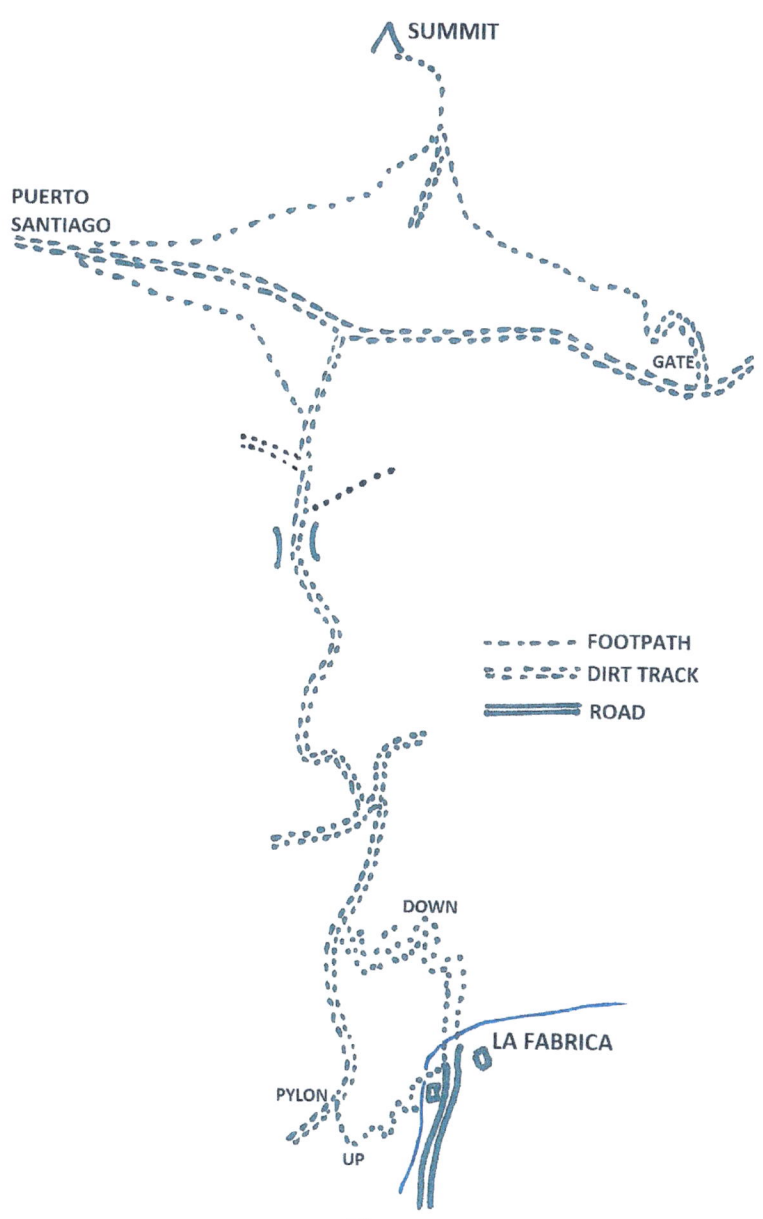

WALK NO. 14

MALAS CAMAS (1,792 METRES) FROM LA FÁBRICA

A long ascent, mainly on broad dirt tracks and a firebreak, to reach a circuit of a lovely high-level plateau and an ascent of one the area's high peaks.

The route can be shortened by a four wheel drive to Los Llanos.

Distance	20 km
Ascent	1,250 metres
Overall grade	Very Strenuous
Terrain	Tracks, firebreaks and footpaths
Exposure	None
Highest point	1,796 metres

The walk begins and ends at La Fábrica de la Luz of Canillas de Albaida. To reach it drive 3 km from the top of Canillas village into the valley, passing a large quarry on the way. Park at the picnic site at La Fábrica.

- Note the ruined building to the left of the track as you arrive at La Fábrica. Immediately beyond it on the left, walk down some steps and cross the stream. A footpath leads up the hill on the far side (going south-west). It zigzags steeply upwards, near a line of electric pylons. It reaches a broad dirt track 180 metres higher up, near one of the pylons. Turn right along the track, going slightly uphill. You will soon pass a gated track going down to the right. Stay on the main track. After about 700 metres from the pylon ignore another major track going down to the right. But make a note of this point, because it is the way back.

- At the next junction of tracks take the right fork. You will be on the right-hand side below the top of a grassy ridge. Then, at a junction with another (major) dirt road, turn left. Very soon you will reach a sharp right-hand bend in the road, where a lesser, stony track goes uphill to the right. (*If you have a four-by-four and want to shorten the walk you may drive to this point. See below for information.*)

- Take this track uphill. It basically follows a firebreak upwards, all the way to the top of the tree-lined ridge ahead. Your target is simply to follow it all the way to the top. It is a more or less continual but steady ascent of 550 metres. The track leaves the firebreak, but returns to join it again at an altitude of 1,300 metres. Here there is a level green clearing. The firebreak continues uphill. A footpath goes off to the right just beyond here, but ignore it. There is then a minor track to the left, leading to a *cortijo*, but it goes no further. So once again ignore it, and continue uphill on the firebreak. Keep going until you reach a fenced area (for the reforestation of yew trees), beyond which you will arrive at a T-junction at a very good dirt track. Turn right along this track for about 1 kilometre of easy walking until you leave the wooded area where a track with a large gate across it goes up to the left.

- Turn left and follow the path round the left-hand side of the gate. Follow the track uphill. It goes right but quickly swings back, so you can take a shortcut. Then follow the track to the right alongside a fence. Below on your right you will see the lovely old semi-ruined *cortijo*, the Haza del Aguadero. Continue on the track, which you will ascend easily, until at a junction of tracks you should turn right and slightly downhill. At this point you will start walking directly towards the peak of Malas Camas, a mass of yellowish-white limestone.

- Continue to a col, where the track swings right to go down towards Haza del Aguadero, but look for a very small cairn on the bend. At the time of writing (2017) there is an arrow made of stones on the ground, pointing the not-so-obvious way to the peak. There are a few small cairns, but it is more of a route than a path. You can choose your own way up. You should be able to see the trig point on the summit. Go straight ahead to reach a level area, and then aim forty-five degrees to the left, more or less directly towards the trig point. The ground is loose and stony, but there is nothing worse than that.

- At the summit you will have great views of La Maroma to the west, La Chapa and El Lucero to the east, the rest of the Sierra Almijara beyond them, and the magnificent Sierra Nevada further east. The reservoir of Los Bermejales can also be seen to the north-east. This is a magnificent view from a remote and little-climbed peak. You will rarely meet any other walkers.

- From the summit return the way you came to the small cairn on the bend in the track. Then go south, back the way you came, and go towards the hilltop ahead, but do not ascend it. Instead take a path to the right, in the direction of La Maroma. The path is overgrown at times, but passable. At a vague junction of paths take the left fork and ascend gradually towards the small ridge above.

- On the ridge top there is a fence, but it is broken down. The objective is to reach the dirt road from Puerto Santiago, which you will see below on the south side of the ridge. There is in fact a gap in the fence at GPS 412466 4083398, and a path goes down beyond it. However, you can descend to the dirt road by whichever route you find easiest. Once there, turn left along the dirt road.

- You now have two options. A minor track leads downhill to the right, going above a *cortijo* where animals are kept, and this track leads back to join the main track that you ascended earlier, below the yew tree plantation. Alternatively you can walk along the main dirt road to reach the top of the firebreak, at which point you can turn right and descend by the route you ascended.

- Much – but not all – of the return route follows the outward route. Descend the firebreak all the way until you meet the main dirt track. Turn left on the track and then next right. Then take the first broad dirt and concrete track on the left, which you passed 700 metres from the pylon. It zigzags down all the way back to La Fábrica, crossing a stream more than once (except in dry seasons). The final task is to cross the main stream, and this is a great place to end a walk as you can soak your aching feet in the cool water.

APPROXIMATE GPS REFERENCES (UTM)

Start	413518 4080210
Pylon	413045 4080057
Top of track down	413091 4080641
Firebreak	413161 4081236
Ignore path	412968 4082151
Top of firebreak	413201 4082991
Gated track	414612 4082842
Keep right on return leg	413574 4083720
Summit	413386 4084097
Path	412137 4083364

NOTE

To shorten the walk by driving part of the way up you will have to drive on dirt roads. I cannot guarantee the condition of these roads, which can vary. To do this, drive from Canillas

WALK NO. 14

de Albaida down the hill towards Árchez, but at a fork on the edge of Canillas go to the right to cross the valley. Pass Finca el Cerrillo. I can't give you full detailed directions here, but you should find your way to El Fogarate and then to la Cruz del Muerto, where you should turn right. Stay on this broad track for some distance until you reach some farm buildings just below on the right, and park anywhere you can here. The walk goes up a dirt track to the left.

Alternatively just ask somebody for directions to Fogarate and then to Cortijo Los Llanos.

Cueva del Melero, Honeymaker's Cave – **WALK 13**

EL LUCERO FROM LA FÁBRICA DE LA LUZ

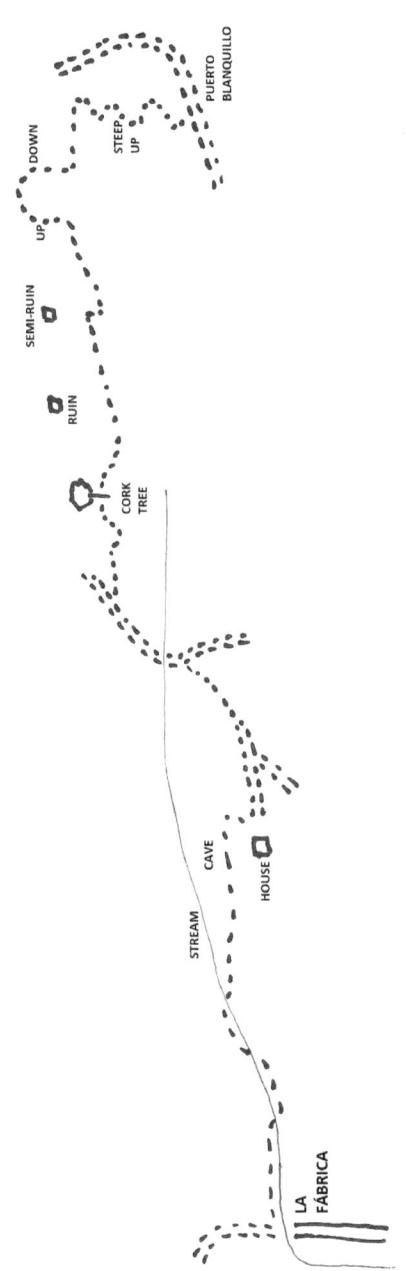

WALK NO. 15

WALK NO. 15 & 16 - EL LUCERO FROM LA FÁBRICA DE LA LUZ & CIRCUIT FROM PUERTO BLANQUILLO

WALK NO. 15

EL LUCERO (1,764 METRES) FROM LA FÁBRICA DE LA LUZ

A linear walk to the most emblematic peak of the Sierra Almijara.

Distance	22 km return trip
Ascent	1,400 metres
Overall grade	Very Strenuous
Terrain	Tracks and footpaths
Exposure	Minimal
Highest point	1,764 metres

The walk can be shortened by driving to Puerto Blanquillo. It reduces the walk to 12 km and 850 metres of ascent but it involves a forty-minute drive, preferably in a four-by-four, on a rough dirt road with drops to one side. See the notes at the end of this walk description for directions to Puerto Blanquillo by car.

From the top of Canillas de Albaida drive to the picnic site at La Fábrica de la Luz and park.

- After arriving by car at La Fábrica walk straight ahead and cross the stream wherever you can. Turn right and follow the path on the far bank. It crosses the stream three more times. Then, as you ascend with the river below on your left, you will pass through some walnut terraces and see the Honeymaker's Cave on the far side. Pass below a farmhouse (where dogs may bark). Beyond the house follow the path up to the right, and reach a track by a gate. Turn left along the track..

- Ignore another track going up to the right and keep straight ahead. The track becomes a path, then joins a track that is part concrete and part dirt. Follow the track up to the left. As it ascends steeply, look for a path starting by some cairns and with an arrow pointing to the right. Follow the path. You will reach a large cork tree by a low wall and a fence at the chestnut farm of El Chaparral. Continue on the path beyond the cork tree. At the foot of a dip in the path do not turn right to cross the watercourse, but go slightly to the left and continue up the valley bottom.

- You will pass the ruined Cortijo Camacho above to your left. The path ascends and then reaches a small farm compound with a smaller cork tree, where the farmer grows artichokes and other crops. The ruined farmhouse is above to the left. Keep going straight ahead, and cross a small watercourse. The path now goes more steeply uphill and becomes sandy. It levels out, only to ascend to the left and then descend to the right once more. It crosses the watercourse (which is usually dry here) for the last time, and continues contouring along the lower slopes of a hillside.

- Soon the sandy and stony path becomes a series of zigzags and ascends very steeply to the right, to reach a broad dirt road. Turn left along the road for about 200 metres and you will reach Puerto Blanquillo (the White Pass).

- At Puerto Blanquillo, where the track swings left, walk straight ahead up a steep path of loose white stones and sand. The path zigzags, sometimes steeply, through a rocky area. As it swings to the right and levels out another path joins it from the right. (At this point you are in the higher reaches of the old Silk Route from Granada to Cómpeta.) Stay on the path to the left, along a level area. Then go slightly uphill to the left into some pine trees, where you should swing right again. Swing sharply right uphill at this bend. Do not go down the left, and also ignore a vague path going ahead into pine forest.

EL LUCERO FROM LA FÁBRICA DE LA LUZ

- Follow the path to the top of the hill, to reach the Puerto de Cómpeta (the Cómpeta Pass). Here you are leaving the province of Málaga and entering that of Granada. On a clear day you will have a good view of the Sierra Nevada (Spain's highest mainland range of hills) straight ahead.

- Continue ahead and descend the path, with a disused marble quarry to your right. At a dirt track turn left to go through some quarry buildings. At a fork in the track turn right and go downhill. After about 0.5 of a kilometre look for a signpost to El Lucero on the right. Turn right by the sign, cross a dry watercourse, and take a good path – which goes to the left, and which rises gently at first. It takes you easily uphill east-south-east, and then swings further south and gets steeper. There are no turns off the path, so continue on it.

- You will reach a level area. Then the path ascends again to another level area before swinging to the left. Make an ascent through some pine trees and you will reach a col among the trees, from where you will see the peak of El Lucero ahead. A very spectacular sight it is, El Lucero being a classic pyramid-shaped peak. This place is commonly known as Base Camp.

- Note the ruined building on the summit of El Lucero. It was an outpost for the *franquistas* in the Spanish Civil War. The building is gradually disappearing. There is a stony mule trail to the top, built for military purposes, which makes the ascent less daunting than it may appear. From Base Camp follow the path downhill to the right, then left on to a col. It then goes up towards a gap between the hill on your right and the main summit. In this gap the path crosses another narrow col, which is the only exposed section of the walk. For just three or four paces it is a little airy, but the path is good and there is no real danger unless you have severe vertigo.

- From this col the stony path continues in multiple zigzags to the summit, where the ruin provides some shade and shelter from winds (and will continue to do so until it disappears entirely). It therefore makes a good picnic stop.

- Return by the way you came. There is an alternative route, which is much more strenuous. It is detailed in Walk 16. To find your way back the normal way, descend to the lower of the two cols, ascend to Base Camp, then turn left to follow the good path downhill to reach the dirt track that leads to the left back to the marble quarry. Go past the quarry buildings. The track turns to the left, and then look for a path up to the right, which will take you over the Puerto de Cómpeta and back to Puerto Blanquillo.

- At Puerto Blanquillo go downhill on the broad track, and after about 200 metres take the steep path down into the valley bottom. Follow the valley all the way back to the start.

APPROXIMATE GPS REFERENCES (UTM)

Start	413518 4080210
Puerto Blanquillo	417359 4080727
Puerto de Cómpeta	417796 4081262
Leave the track	418552 4081380
Base Camp	419709 4080697
Summit	420620 4080548

TO START FROM PUERTO BLANQUILLO

Starting here the walk becomes considerably easier, with total ascent of 850 metres and a return distance of only 11 km. This walk has a moderate grading, but you will need a four-by-four vehicle to reach the start of the walk.

EL LUCERO FROM LA FÁBRICA DE LA LUZ

From Santa Ana, at the top of Canillas, drive on the road signposted towards La Fábrica. At a fork in the road keep right. Then, where the asphalt road swings sharply to the right, keep straight on along a dirt road. Stay on this dirt track for about thirty minutes, ignoring a turn-off to the right after a few minutes, and later ignoring another turn to the left with a chain across. In short, stay on the main track. Be very careful. Sometimes parts of the road get washed away, and there is no barrier at the side. When the road widens and the rocks become very white, at about 11 km from the village, the track swings sharp left to skirt the top of the valley. This is Puerto Blanquillo. Park here.

La Maroma from the Guardia post on El Lucero –
WALK 15

WALK NO. 16

EL LUCERO – CIRCUIT FROM PUERTO BLANQUILLO

A route to the peak of El Lucero (1,764 metres), going out on the 'classic' ascent, and returning via a more difficult and remote route.

Distance	13 km
Ascent	950 metres
Overall grade	Very Strenuous
Terrain	Footpaths and some rough ground
Exposure	Minimal
Highest point	1,764 metres

The walk begins and ends at Puerto Blanquillo.

This route is more strenuous than the more normal route as it involves a steep downhill section, followed by repeated ascents and descents along a path below the south face of the hills.

The start of the walk at Puerto Blanquillo is reached by driving 11 kilometres on a dirt road that can be rough at times. It can be done in a normal car with care, but is much more suitable for a sturdy four-wheel drive.

For the route to the summit follow Walk 15. This is a description of the second part of the walk.

- From the summit, descend on the zigzag path you have already ascended. Cross the first col to where the path descends on the right-hand slopes of the subsidiary peak, and continue on a clear stony path. Shortly before the lowest point on a broad ridge (at GPS 420009 4080564) turn left and walk down a loose, sandy path into a shallow gully. This is not an easy stretch. Keep going down and you will reach a watercourse, which is usually dry. Follow the watercourse downhill to the right. After 50 metres or so, as the watercourse continues to descend, look for a path to the right that is marked by cairns. Follow the path for the next hour below the south face of the hills. You will repeatedly descend and ascend again to cross several ridges, sometimes among pine trees, sometimes in the open.

- Although the path is indistinct at times, once you are on it there are no alternatives, so stick at it and you will find your way. The route is remote and spectacular. It can be difficult in places, due to erosion and fallen trees.

- After a zigzag descent through pinewoods, followed by yet another ascent to the top of a ridge, the path descends again to cross an open stretch of land. At the far side of this open area, and about 3 kilometres from where you joined this path, a few more zigzags will lead you uphill to join a good path, which comes up the hillside from the left. Turn right along this path and follow it uphill. Soon going over a small col the path levels out. Then ignore a path going down to the left and continue uphill. You will soon see the white stony track at Puerto Blanquillo below to the left.

- When Puerto Blanquillo comes into sight there is a minor path, which will take you directly back to the start of the walk at the risk of a few more gorse scratches. Alternatively you can carry on uphill until you join the path you ascended on the outward route. Turn left and back to the start. This latter option is clearer, but involves somewhat more distance and more ascent.

WALK NO. 16

APPROXIMATE GPS REFERENCES (UTM)

Start	417359 4080727
"Base Camp"	419709 4080697
Summit	420620 4080548
Steep path down	420009 4080564
Watercourse	419790 4080418
Right turn	417705 4079921
Do not turn left	417537 4080353

Path to El Lucero – **WALK 16**

WALK NO. 17 - THE SILK ROUTE AND LA FÁBRICA

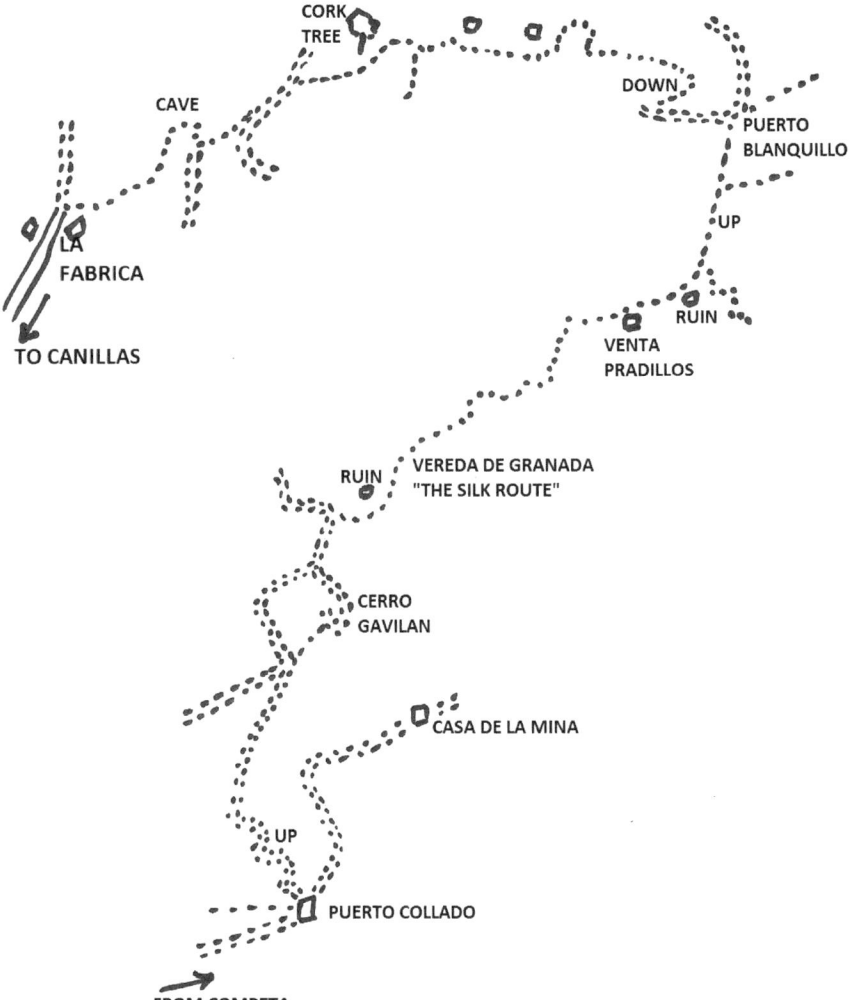

WALK NO. 17

THE SILK ROUTE AND LA FÁBRICA

A linear walk from a viewpoint above Cómpeta, via the Silk Route path, to a delightful picnic area by a stream near Canillas de Albaida.

Distance	14 km linear
Ascent	570 metres
Overall grade	Moderate
Terrain	Footpaths and dirt tracks
Exposure	None
Highest point	1,214 metres

The walk begins at Puerto Collado, a magnificent viewpoint 2 kilometres from Cómpeta. It can be reached by driving along a dirt road signposted from the higher parts of Cómpeta towards Casa de la Mina. If you prefer you can start the walk in Cómpeta, which will add 2.5 kilometres of distance and 300 metres of ascent to the walk.

The walk ends at La Fábrica de la Luz of Canillas de Albaida, a well-known beauty spot 3 km from the village at the end of a tarmac road. You can order a taxi to pick you up here, or walk to the village if you prefer.

- To walk from Cómpeta, from the main square by the church, take any of the labyrinthine streets, uphill and easterly, to reach a ring road around the top of the town. Look for a concrete road uphill signposted towards Casa de la Mina. At the top turn left near a shrine, and follow the road uphill and then to the right below Cruz del Monte, a housing development. The dirt road swings right not far from the shrine.

- Higher up the hill the track passes a solitary house on the right and swings left again. Continue round some more bends, and then continue further on a straight stretch to reach a fabulous viewpoint at Puerto Collado. This whole area was badly burnt by wildfire in 2014 and will take some time to recover. But the views are still great.

- The view from the *mirador* (viewpoint) includes Nerja on the coast, and the Sierra Almijara is ahead. The *puerto* (at 890 metres above sea level) is a junction of three dirt roads. Walk up the dirt track uphill to the north (turning sharp left as you come up from Cómpeta). It ascends in zigzags. Eventually it levels out, and you will see Cómpeta way below on the left. Continue on the level track to reach a pylon at the foot of the hill of Cerro Gavilán. Here you have a choice. The easier route is to stay on the dirt track skirting the left flank of the hill. The more interesting route is to go straight ahead up the hill, where a footpath takes you across some rocky outcrops to reach another dirt road, just beyond which is the fire control post at the summit of Gavilán (1,133 metres). There are spectacular views in all directions.

- From the summit follow the dirt track descending the hill in a semi-spiral. It soon rejoins the lower track some distance from where you left it. Continue on this track to a junction at Cruz de Canillas, where a footpath heads off to the right (north-east).

- This path is officially the Vereda de Granada, or the animal trail to Granada. But locally it is known as the Silk Route. It was used as a trading route by muleteers from Moorish times until the late twentieth century. In its day it was the main road from Cómpeta to Granada. Turn right along it, and almost immediately you will pass an inn (the Venta de Maria Guerrero), which has been in ruins since the Spanish Civil War. Continue on the path, sometimes on the level and at times undulating, until half an hour further on you reach a second ruined inn, the Venta de Pradillos. At the far side of the buildings there is an old *era*. The path goes slightly to the left from the *era*. A little farther on there is an old limepit and then a third ruined inn, the Venta de Cándido.

- Continue on the main path past the ruin. Ignore a turn-off downhill to the right. The path swings to the left and ascends alongside a watercourse (which is normally dry). At a junction marked with cairns go straight ahead (the Silk Route turns right here). Stay in the watercourse, and ascend on stony and sandy ground to reach the pass of Puerto Blanquillo, where you will meet a major dirt track.

- Turn left along the track for about 200 metres and look for cairns on the right that indicate a footpath going downhill, very steeply at first, into the bottom of the valley. Follow this path all the way to the valley floor. (Walking poles will be helpful here.)

- The path is now very sandy. It goes gradually downhill above a dry stream bed (which flows after heavy rain) and eventually crosses the stream to the right bank, where you should take care not to follow the stream any further. The path heads uphill again to the right, to cross a rocky bluff. Then descend once more to the level of the stream.

- You will reach a semi-ruined farm. The path keeps to the left before the house, crosses a minor watercourse, and then continues along the valley below the house and to the right of an irrigated patch of farmland with a cork tree. Keep on the main path, which crosses an area of barren landscape. Do not cross the watercourse. Stay just to the right of the valley bottom until you reach a large cork tree at the chestnut farm of El Chaparral.

- Continue along the path and then down a dirt/concrete track, zigzagging down to reach the valley floor once more. The dirt track swings to the left and starts to ascend. Leave the track at the valley floor, go straight on to rejoin the footpath, and cross the stream, which may not be flowing here (the water gradually emerges as you descend the valley). The path soon gives way to a broader track, which you should follow until you reach a junction. Take the right fork.

- At a farm gate turn sharp right. Do not enter the farmyard unless you want trouble with dogs. The path goes down to the right and then immediately left below the farmhouse (the Cortijo del Chato), with the Honeymaker's Cave opposite on the right. Follow the path through walnut terraces and on to cross the stream (now in full flow) four times. The last time will be at La Fábrica de la Luz, a wonderful place to end a walk, where you can remove your boots and dangle your feet in the water in sunshine or in the shade of the trees.

- *From La Fábrica, the easiest way back to Cómpeta or Canillas is by taxi. You can walk to Canillas in 3 km, but most of it is on tarmac. There is very little traffic, but you have to pass a limestone quarry on the way. If you decide to walk, once you are past the quarry ignore a minor turn to the right and go on until you reach a T-junction of roads. Turn right and then look for a track going uphill to the left. This leads, within 50 metres, to an irrigation canal, which you can follow all the way to Canillas, high up above the road. It is more pleasant than road walking, but it is somewhat airy and involves a bit of exposure. It may not suit those with vertigo, who should stay on the road.*

WALK NO. 17

APPROXIMATE GPS REFERENCES (UTM)

Start	415009 4076622
Silk Route path	415236 4078658
Venta de Pradillos	416716 4079703
Puerto Blanquillo	417360 4080723
Path down	417160 4080839
La Fábrica	413518 4080210

El Fuerte, Frigiliana and the sea seen from – **WALK 17**

PUERTO COLLADO TO CASA DE LA MINA AND THE SILK ROUTE

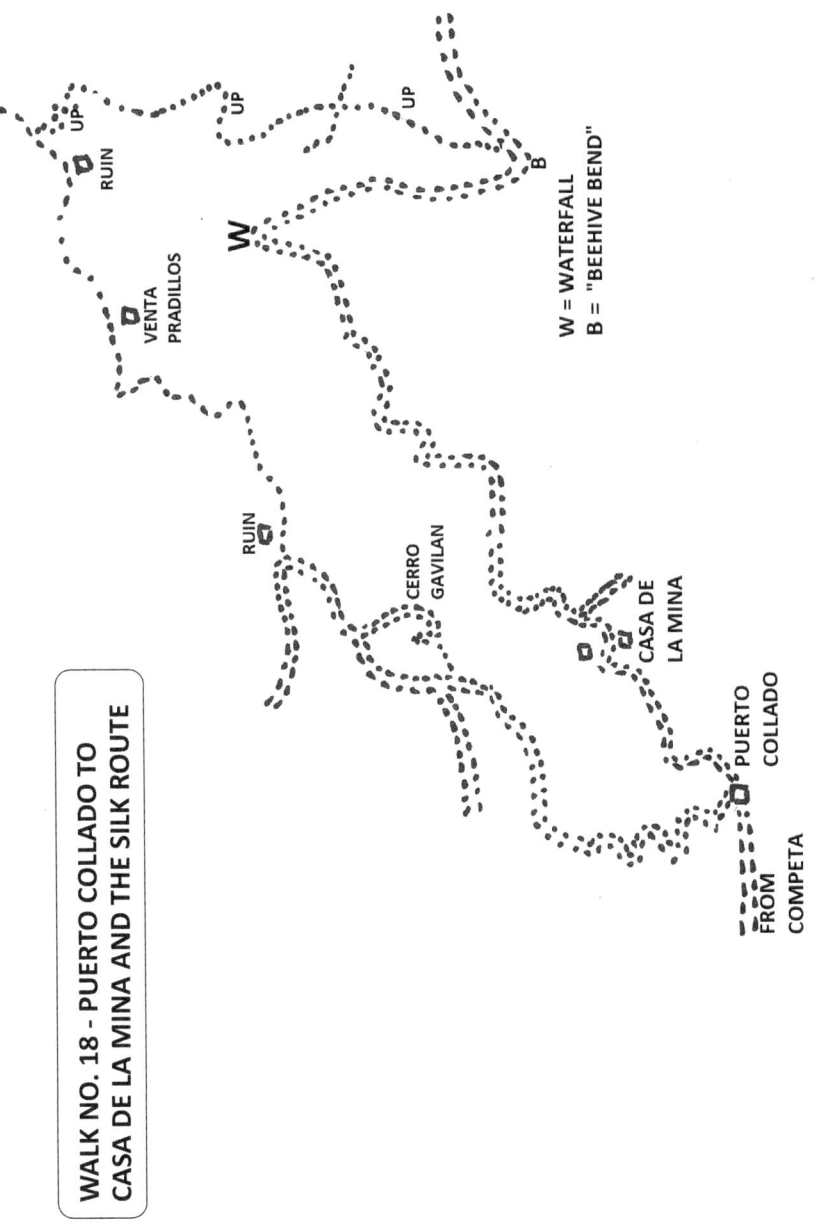

WALK NO. 18

PUERTO COLLADO TO CASA DE LA MINA AND THE SILK ROUTE

A circular walk from above Cómpeta, via Casa de la Mina, Venta de Pradillos and the Silk Route.

This circular walk covers part of Walk 17, but in reverse, and allows for starting and finishing in the same place.

Distance	14 km
Ascent	450 metres
Overall grade	Moderate
Terrain	Footpaths and dirt tracks
Exposure	None
Highest point	1,138 metres

The walk begins and ends at Puerto Collado, a magnificent viewpoint 2 kilometres from Cómpeta. Puerto Collado can be reached by driving along a good dirt road signposted from the higher parts of Cómpeta towards Casa de la Mina.

If you prefer you can start and end the walk in Cómpeta, which will add 5 kilometres of distance and 300 metres of ascent to the walk.

- To walk from Cómpeta to Puerto Collado, follow the directions in Walk 17.
- At Puerto Collado (890 metres above sea level) a dirt road goes uphill to the left, but ignore it and walk along the next dirt road, going gradually downhill. After 2 kilometres of easy walking you will arrive at the Casa la Mina, where a modern but more or less abandoned hotel is on the left and the original hostel is on the right. You may find a bar open here for coffee, but don't bank on it.

- Continue beyond the hotel, staying on the main track and ignoring a track going down to the right. Follow the track for approximately a further 3 kilometres, during which you will descend gradually (a total descent of about 50 metres from the start of the walk). At the lowest point, where the track swings to the right and uphill, you will find a small green valley on the left, where a stream crosses the dirt road. In the valley you will find a little waterfall. This is a good place for a rest.

- Continue on the main track, now uphill, for a further kilometre, until at the top of an incline it swings sharply to the left. I call this point Beehive Bend, due to the beehives in the fields beyond.

- Go just around the bend, and straight away take a footpath ascending to the left that goes towards a steep ridge. The path ascends on to a firebreak, and after a short distance it leaves the firebreak and takes a route to the left, staying well below the crest of the ridge.

- The ascent is through woodland and scrub. Continue on the path, which after a steep climb levels out and then takes a turn up to the right. It very soon swings to the left again, and ascends another short steep stretch to a rocky area before levelling out once more.

- While walking along on a level stretch, and even slightly downhill at times, you will pass a pile of stones (a land boundary, not a cairn) and then descend to the left to cross a watercourse. On the far side the path goes very steeply uphill in zigzags for a short distance, and reaches the Vereda de Granada (also known as the Silk Route, the old trading mule trail to Granada). Turn left along this good-quality path.

- After just two or three minutes you will reach the Venta de Cándido, a ruined inn. Shortly beyond the inn you will find an old *calero* (a limepit for making *cal*, which is the whitewash they used to use for houses). The path – which is now stony – descends, and after a few minutes reaches the *era* at the side of the next ruined inn, the Venta de Pradillos. This is a great place for a picnic, with views down to Torrox on the coast.

- Go the far end of the ruins. The path continues, sometimes downhill, sometimes uphill, but generally following the contours of the hillside. It swings to the left and then soon swings to the right, and rises to a level area. Then it continues to undulate, and after a further ten minutes' walk or so it rises, going to the right-hand side of a rocky area with some prominent large pine trees.

- Continue on the path to reach the third and final ruined inn, the Venta de Maria Guerrero. Shortly after the *venta* the path reaches a junction with a dirt road, where you should turn left towards the fire watch station on the summit of Cerro Gavilán. At the foot of the hill you can choose to either ascend the concrete track to the summit (see Walk 12) or preferably take the easier route, staying on the track past the right side of the hill. Continue on the track to reach a pylon at a junction of tracks.

- Near the pylon another path goes steeply down to the left. Ignore that path and take the left fork of the two main tracks. It stays on the level at first then goes just slightly uphill. Swing to the left on to a level stretch, with Cómpeta below on the right, and then go down the zigzag track to return to Puerto Collado. There are several shortcuts along the track, on steep and loose ground.

APPROXIMATE GPS REFERENCES (UTM)

Puerto Collado	415009 4076612
Waterfall	416805 4079297
Beehive Bend	416940 4078577
Silk Route path	417151 4079887

PUERTO COLLADO TO CASA DE LA MINA AND THE SILK ROUTE

Turn left	415232 4078648
Left fork on the track	414963 4077799

Approaching Puerta de Frigiliana – **WALK 19**

WALK NO. 19

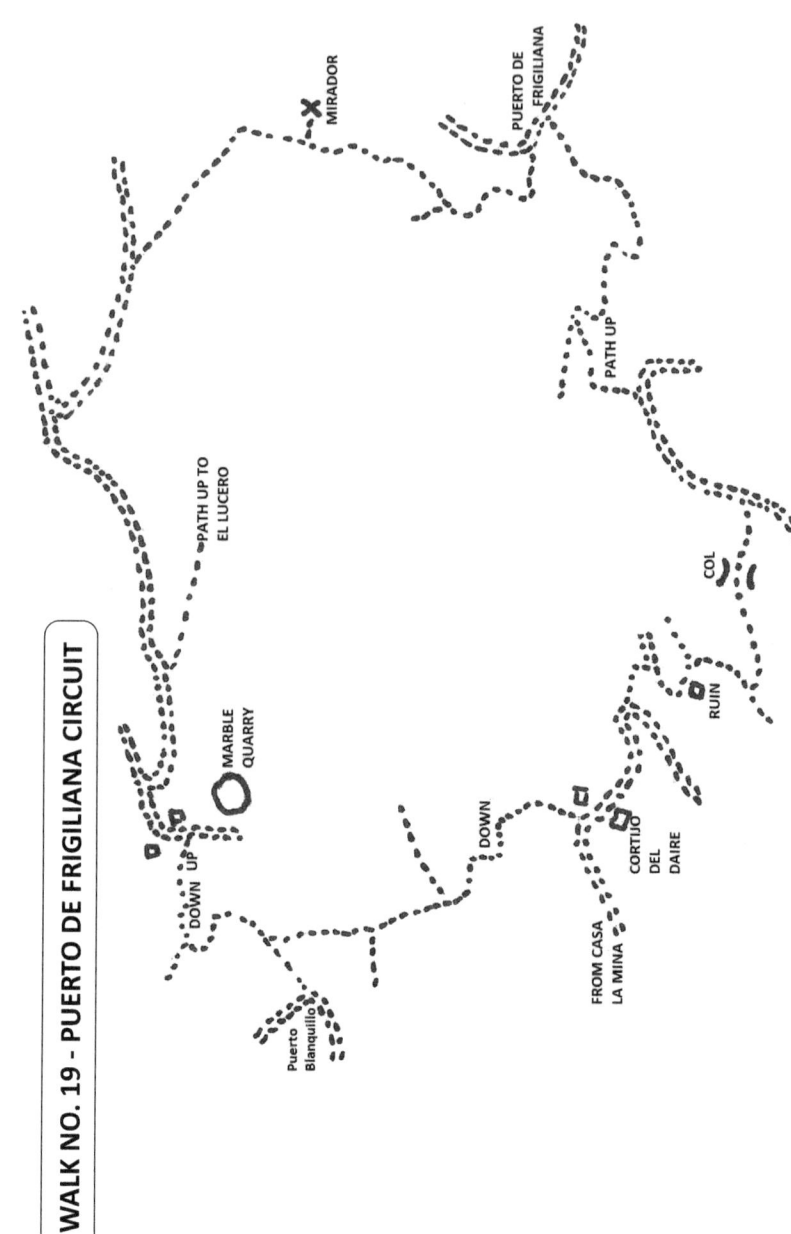

WALK NO. 19

PUERTO DE FRIGILIANA CIRCUIT

A circular walk from the ruined Cortijo del Daire, via Puerto de Frigiliana and the north side of El Lucero.

Distance	17.5 km
Ascent	1,050 metres
Overall grade	Strenuous
Terrain	Footpaths and a dirt track
Exposure	None
Highest point	1,417 metres

The El Daire ruin is reached by a lengthy drive on a dirt road. It can be done in an ordinary car with care, but a four-by-four is very much preferable.

Driving directions:

Drive from Cómpeta to Casa de la Mina and then keep straight on. Ignore any turn-offs to the right. The dirt road twists and turns for approximately 6 kilometres beyond Casa de la Mina. There is ample parking space near the ruined inn. Take care along here, since the dirt road is entirely unfenced and will not suit nervous drivers.

Walk along the dirt road going north-east from the El Daire ruin. After 0.75 km the track crosses a watercourse and swings to the right. Leave the road here and go straight ahead, where a vague footpath takes you slightly uphill and then to the right. It can be a little prickly with brambles here. Continue up the path, ignore another track going left into a valley, and continue to reach a ruin.

- Go to the far left hand side of the ruin and take a path downhill and to the right. It crosses a little valley and goes round to the far side of a rise, but still in the valley, as the path starts to ascend, look for some cairns on the left marking the start of an indistinct (at first) path. It goes uphill towards the ridge above. Follow the path to the crest of the ridge and continue down the far side.

- The path is a good one until it reaches a narrow watercourse. When you reach it do not descend the watercourse, but look for a cairn on the far side marking a continuation of the path, which now becomes somewhat overgrown. Follow it downhill to reach a dirt road, and turn left along it. You will soon cross two watercourses, and just beyond the second one take a path sharply to the left that is marked by cairns.

- This path leads steadily uphill, keeping to the right of the stream Barranco del Atajo. At a junction keep right. The path will lead you into another valley, and then more or less up the centre of this *barranco*. At one point a vague red arrow shows the path ascending to the right, but the path soon comes back into the gully, so if you miss the arrow it is not disastrous.

- Continue on the path until it emerges at the top of the gully at Puerto de Frigiliana (the Frigiliana Pass). Turn left along a broad dirt track for a few metres to where a sign tells you about the nature of this place. The views are excellent.

- A good footpath begins near the signpost, going to the west at first and then towards the mountain of El Lucero. However, it soon veers to the north and begins a route that circuits the eastern flank of the mountain. Where a path goes to the left (marked with green paint) ignore it and keep right. Stay on the path until it reaches a viewpoint on the right(the Mirador del Agua) and continue until you reach a broader dirt track. Turn left along the track. When it meets another (even broader) track, turn left again and follow it all the way to the disused marble quarry below Puerto de Cómpeta.

- Go through the quarry buildings, and then almost immediately take a path up to the right to reach the *puerto*. Continue on the path down the far side of the pass. It swings left in pinewoods then goes to the right on a level stretch, at the far end of which a post marks the start of a path to the left. Take the left turn.
- While walking along this path you will see Puerto Blanquillo below to the right, but stay high. Ignore any paths going down to the right. Cross a col, and then start a descent towards the El Daire ruin. Ignore a good path going to the left. Keep descending. Do not take a track into the valley to the left. Stay on the main path going south-east to return to the start of the walk.

APPROXIMATE GPS REFERENCES (UTM)

Cortijo del Daire	418191 4079377
Ruin	418747 4078967
Collado los Civiles	419686 4079404
Puerto de Frigiliana	421608 4079656
Mirador	420777 4081708
Main track	419890 4082098
Path left	417457 4080915

WALK NO. 20

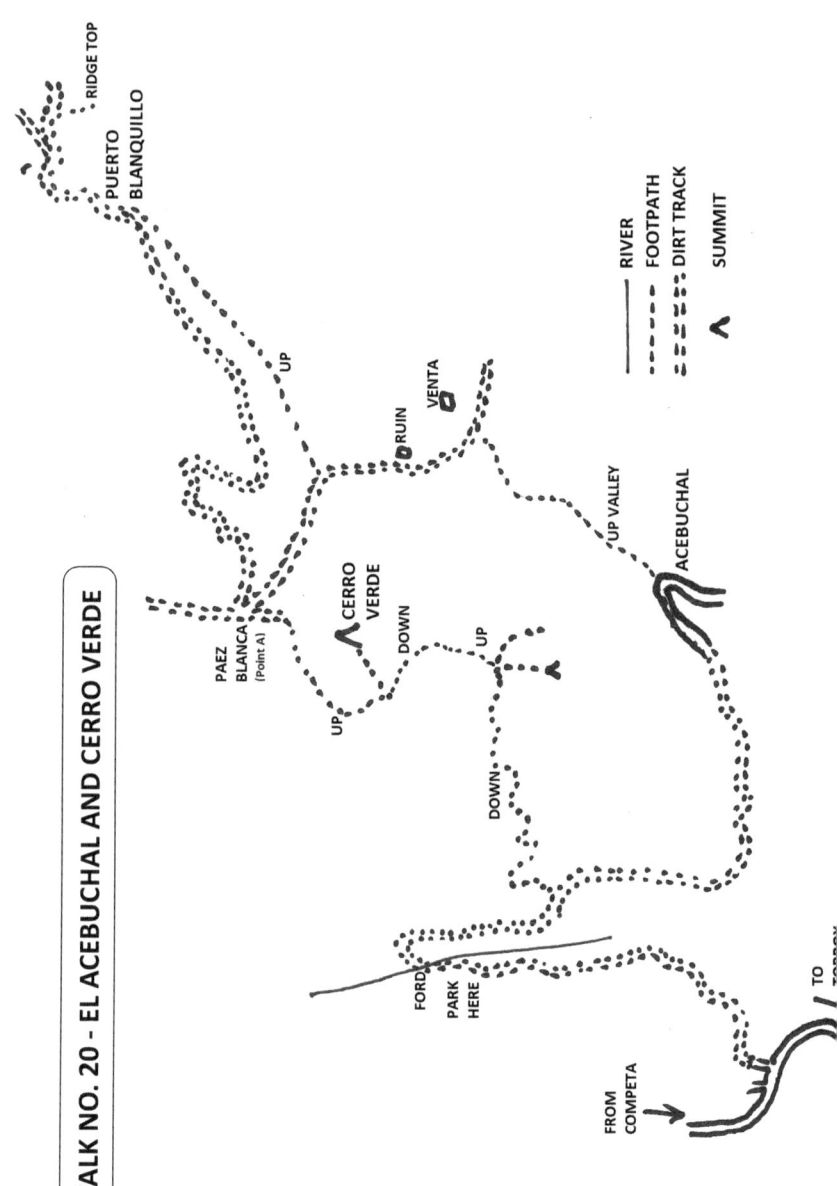

WALK NO. 20

EL ACEBUCHAL AND CERRO VERDE

A circular route from near Cómpeta via the remote hamlet of El Acebuchal.

Distance	17 km
Ascent	660 metres
Overall grade	Strenuous
Terrain	Footpaths and dirt tracks
Exposure	None
Highest point	1,050 metres

Drive from Cómpeta on the Torrox road for about 4 km until you reach a sharp bend at the bottom of the hill, where the road starts a broad sweep to the right. (If you reach the Hotel Pavo Real you have gone too far.) As you reach the bend there are dirt roads going to the left. Take the first of these. Do not ascend a concrete strip, but stay on the dirt track that goes below and to the right of it. The track is generally well surfaced, but go slowly so that you don't ground your car. Continue on the track going gradually downhill until you reach a ford over the river. Park anywhere here to start the walk. This is La Fábrica de la Luz de Cómpeta (not to be confused with La Fábrica de la Luz of Canillas).

- Walk across the river. You may have to paddle, but it is not very deep except after heavy rain. Once across the river follow the track, and then almost immediately turn right at a junction. Follow this track gently uphill. At 1.4 kilometres from the start of the walk you will pass a narrow path on the left, but for now ignore it. (It is the return route.) Continue along the track, and at 3.5 km from the start of the walk you will arrive at the small, remote village of El Acebuchal, where you should be able to get a coffee at one of its two bars, which are virtually next door to each other.

- El Acebuchal was a ruined village until about the year 2000, when it was rebuilt. Its history is connected to the Spanish Civil War. It was in virtually total ruins from 1949 to the turn of the twenty-first century.

- Continue to the far (north-eastern) end of the village. Leave the track where it swings back to the right and continue straight ahead, up a watercourse. It is marked (with red and white bands on a post) as part of the long-distance route GR 242/GR 249. At times the path leaves the valley bottom, but it soon rejoins it. About 1.5 km into the walk you can either follow the path ascending to the left or stay in the valley bottom. Either way a steepish ascent leads you to a dirt track near a signpost saying *Venta de Cebollera*.

- Turn left, following the main track. You will soon reach a ruin with a signpost saying *Venta de Cebollera*. Continue up the track to reach a fork, where you should take the right fork (but take the left fork for a shortcut, which will take you to Point A on the sketch map). The right fork was signposted *Puerta Verde but at the time of writing the sign has fallen down*. This track/stream valley/footpath leads gradually uphill, with no real difficulties, until it joins a major dirt track at Puerto Blanquillo.

- Our route goes to the left here, but the best bit of the walk is to the right. So, on reaching the track, turn right, and you will almost immediately see the twin-peaked mountain of El Cisne (The Swan) ahead. A little further on you will see the peak of El Lucero ahead and to the left. You can retrace your steps here. But it is best to go on for a kilometre more, to a point where the track forks. Take the right fork, and after just a few metres turn right on to a footpath going along a ridge. Walk along the path for just a few metres to where there are great views. This makes a good destination for the walk, and a good place for a rest.

- Retrace your steps to Puerto Blanquillo. Ignore the path you ascended and stay on the higher level track, which after many bends leads to another junction of tracks at Paez Blanca (Point A on the map, where the shortcut comes in).

- Here a major track goes to the right and another goes downhill to the left. Take the track going ahead, slightly uphill and slightly to the left. Then ignore another track going to the left. You now have views back down towards the Cómpeta Fábrica. The track skirts the western slopes of Cerro Verde and soon becomes a narrow footpath.

- The path ascends steadily up the flank of the hill. When it reaches the crest of the ridge, there are some cairns where you can turn left for 500 metres of distance and 140 metres of ascent to reach the summit of Cerro Verde. From the summit return to the crest of the ridge and the cairns. Turn left (south) along the path, which descends a little along the eastern flank of the hill. Soon El Acebuchal will come into view way below. The path ascends again and goes to the right to reach a col, where there is a junction of paths.

- A path to the left goes down to El Acebuchal. The path straight ahead just goes to the small hill directly ahead of you and no further. But the path downhill to the right is the return route to La Fábrica. It goes downhill steeply at times and through lots of undergrowth, mainly rosemary. It can be a little prickly, but at the time of writing it is quite passable.

- There are no options here. Just follow the twists and turns in the path, and keep a keen eye open to make sure you do not lose it. The path descends to eventually meet the broad track near the start. Turn right on the track for 1.4 km.

APPROXIMATE GPS REFERENCES (UTM)

Start	416016 4076209
Ignore path to left	416280 4075452
El Acebuchal start of path	417646 4075102
Path to right	418249 4076306
Turning point	419732 4077716
Paez Blanca (Point A)	417580 4076940
Col	417159 4076154
Path down	416921 4075775

NOTE:

If you wish to take a shorter route, drive to El Acebuchal in order to begin and end the walk there. From Frigiliana most of the road is concrete, but from Cómpeta there is some rough dirt track and you have to cross the ford, so a sturdy car is necessary. This route saves about 5 kilometres of distance and makes for a moderate walk.

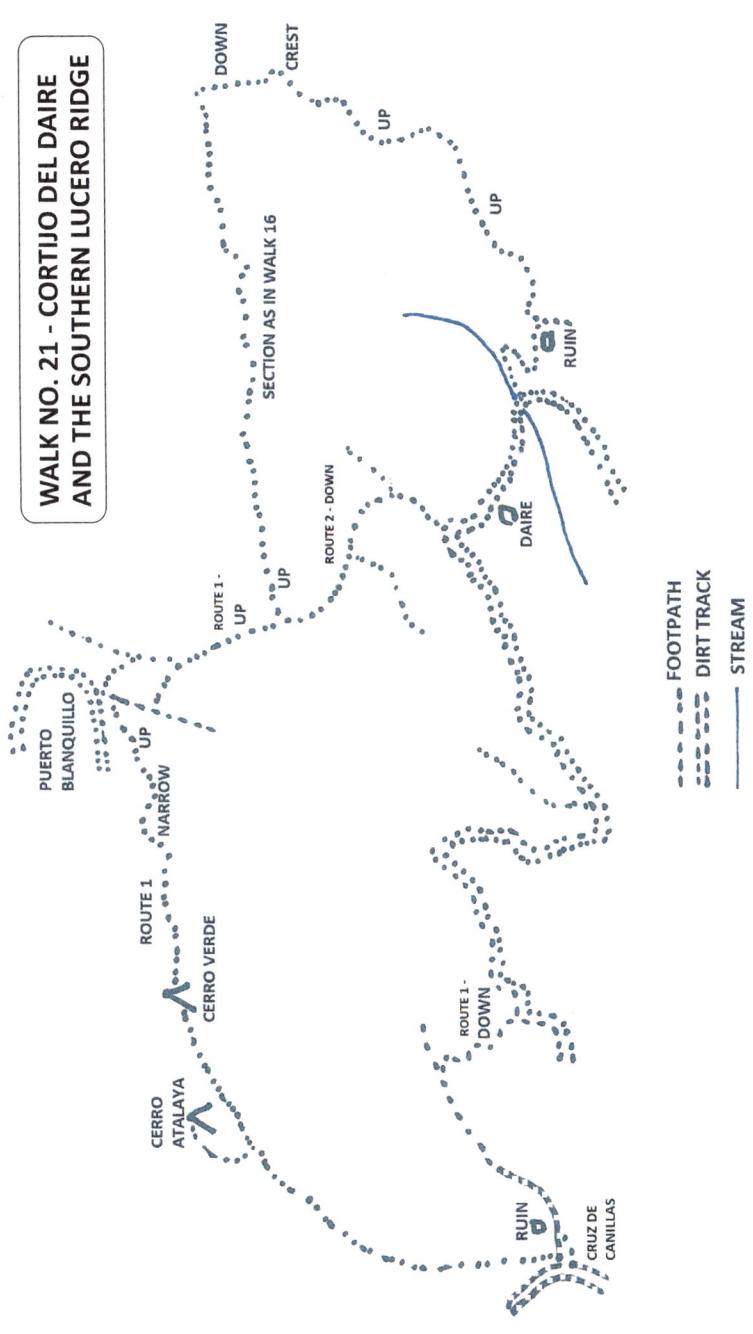

WALK NO. 21

CORTIJO DEL DAIRE AND THE SOUTHERN LUCERO RIDGE

A walk via the ruined El Daire inn, ascending the southern ridge of El Lucero.

There are two versions of this walk: one moderate, one very strenuous. Route 1 returns at high level, and includes a part of Walk 13. Route 2 is shorter, but more remote. Both routes include part of the return path from El Lucero (Walk 16). Despite the repetition of some sections of path, each of these in total is a new route.

ROUTE 1 Distance	19 km
Ascent	1,500 metres
Overall grade	Very Strenuous
Terrain	Footpaths and a dirt track
Exposure	There is one short, narrow stretch of path above a steep, stony slope.
Highest point	1,440 metres

ROUTE 2 Distance	9 km
Ascent	800 metres
Overall grade	Moderate
Terrain	Mainly good footpaths
Exposure	A high ridge but with no real exposure
Highest point	1,440 metres

The ridge can be seen from a distance. It is on the southern flanks of El Lucero, and has a jagged rocky outline with pine trees in the depressions. The path can be seen making a zigzag ascent up the flanks of the ridge. It looks formidable, but it is not as severe as it appears.

The Cortijo del Daire is one of the old inns that have been in ruins since the Civil War of the 1930s.

Route 1 begins at Cruz de Canillas. To get there by car you ideally need a four-by-four. Drive from Canillas de Albaida from the Santa Ana chapel towards La Fábrica de la Luz. At a fork keep right. When the surfaced road swings sharp right go straight ahead on a bumpy dirt road. Keep going for just over 2 kilometres. Where the road swings sharp left take a right turn. Go uphill for another 2 km to where the road levels and swings sharp right. Park here, at the start of the Silk Route.

- Set out along the Silk Route, as in Walk 17. Pass the first ruin and continue on the path for 1 kilometre (approximately). As the path goes downhill there is a rocky outcrop on the right with a stand of pine trees. Immediately beyond this outcrop look for some cairns on the right and take a path downhill. Follow it round several bends. The path will pass an old *calero* and then reach the dirt road that leads from Casa de la Mina to the El Daire ruin. Turn left along the track and follow it for about 3.5 km of easy walking until you reach the large ruin on the right. (*For Route 2 this where you will start and finish.*)

Route 2 begins at Cortijo del Daire. It is reached by driving for 10 km along a rough dirt road from Cómpeta. A four-wheel drive is preferable. If you go in an ordinary car take it very steadily. The road is narrow and has no barrier. Drive from Cómpeta to Casa de la Mina, and just keep going. Ignore any turn-offs down to the right. When you reach the El Daire ruin there is ample parking.

- From Cortijo del Daire walk along the main dirt track in a south-easterly direction. Ignore a track to the right, and continue for 700 metres from the El Daire ruin. You will cross the Barranco Zarandilla, a stream by a sharp right-hand bend. Do not go round the bend, but instead go straight ahead into a valley on a somewhat overgrown path. You will be on the right-hand side of a stream, and it may be a little overgrown – and possibly a little wet.

- A track takes you to the right. Soon you will meet a junction where a track goes left towards a valley. Ignore it and keep right. The track leads to a ruin. To the left, above a low wall, is an old threshing floor. Take a path starting next to and to the right of the threshing floor. (Do not follow the main track ahead into a valley.) The path ascends to the crest of a broad ridge. As it climbs it takes lots of zigzags and has some steep sections.

- The path leaves the crest of the ridge and begins a traverse to the left across its western flanks. There are no alternative paths up here. Just follow the path. At times it may be indistinct, and there may be fallen trees to be circumnavigated, so keep a sharp eye open for the path.

- The path ascends and returns to the crest of the ridge at the Collado de los Civiles, a rocky col. Continue on the path, going north, just below the ridge crest on its western side. At GPS 419878 4080127 you may find a little confusion in the path. Do not descend the eastern slopes, but look for the path continuing along the ridge top. This is a slightly airy part of the path, although experienced hill walkers will not find it problematic.

- The path leaves the crest of the ridge again, on its western side, and you will cross the head of some steep dry valleys on loose ground, where care is needed to not lose either the path or your footing. There is barren ground between the pine trees, and where to walk is not always obvious. Watch out for the cairns so as to keep to the correct route.

- After a short distance on this terrain you will swing down to the left and enter a more obvious watercourse. Some cairns mark the path a little farther downhill. This is the return route from El Lucero that is described in Walk 16. Leave the watercourse following the cairned path to its right. It ascends and descends repeatedly. After approximately 3 kilometres on this path, and after crossing an open area of land, you will ascend some short zigzags and find another path coming up from the left and continuing up to the right.

- (a) If you are taking Route 2 turn left here and descend this path to the El Daire ruin. On the way do not take a path to the left, which is a dead end. Keep descending along the right-hand side of a valley until you reach the major dirt road, where the El Daire ruin is around the bend to the left. The walk ends here.

- (b) For Route 1 turn right on reaching the path and go uphill. The path levels out and then descends just slightly. Continue, ignoring a path to the left, and continue to Puerto Blanquillo (the White Pass). When you see the *puerto* below to the left, a minor path goes directly to it. If you do not find the minor path don't worry, but continue uphill to reach a major path where you can turn left and descend to the pass.

- Instead of taking the dirt road downhill at the *puerto*, go up the hillside to the left of the road. It is a rocky and sandy slope. You will find a clear, sandy track going to the left, but it is a dead end. So do not take what looks like the obvious path. Instead, scramble up a little higher and look for a path to the left above some dark-coloured rocks. It ascends past some trees and then swings right uphill and into the open. It soon levels out and then crosses an area on loose ground above a steep slope down to the left. *It is not especially difficult, but will not suit those with vertigo.*

- Continue on this path at a high level, with the crest of the hills above to the right. You will reach a col where a path joins from the right, and then you are at the base of Cerro Verde. Keep going on the top of the ridge, cross the top of Cerro Verde, and descend towards Cerro Atalaya, the mountain with a rocky peak ahead. At the col before Atalaya go straight on, passing Atalaya on your right. Do not turn right to ascend the peak, but go straight ahead and the path will lead you back to Cruz de Canillas and the end of the walk.

APPROXIMATE GPS REFERENCES (UTM)

Cruz de Canillas	415232 4078648
Path down (approx)	415884 4079131
Cortijo del Daire	418191 4079377
Barranco Moreno	418691 4079058
Start of path up	418747 4078967
Collado los Civiles	419686 4079404
Top of ridge	419878 4080127
Watercourse and path	419790 4080418
Route 1 or 2 choice	417705 4079921
Puerto Blanquillo	417359 4080727
Path above the *puerto*	417271 4080678
Cerro Verde	415847 4079990
Col beyond Atalaya	415697 4079321

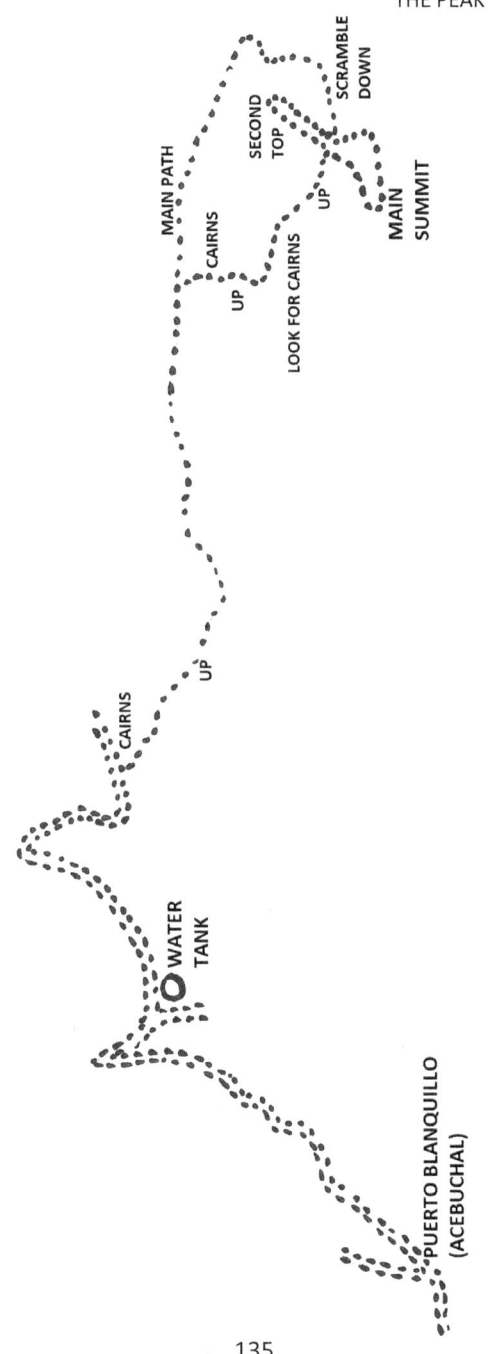

WALK NO. 22

THE PEAK OF EL CISNE (THE SWAN)

A remote and spectacular mountain with two peaks.

The walk is less than 10 km, but with 915 metres of ascent and descent on mainly rough ground. It is steep and strenuous, with some difficult terrain. A great walk for the more adventurous.

Distance	9.5 km
Ascent	915 metres
Overall grade	Strenuous
Terrain	Footpaths, dirt tracks and some stony ground
Exposure	An airy but not difficult scramble to the peak, and a difficult, steep scramble down on slippery ground
Highest point	1,495 metres

The walk begins at Puerto Blanquillo, but there are two places with that name and you must get the right one. This Puerto Blanquillo is the one between Cómpeta and Frigiliana, not the one between Cómpeta and Canillas. To reach it, unless you are a very strong walker, you need to drive there in a four-by-four. (Strong walkers can reach it from El Acebuchal by following the first part of Walk 23.)

This is how to get to Puerto Blanquillo by four wheel drive:

From Cómpeta take the dirt road to Casa de la Mina (signposted from the eastern end of Cómpeta). At Casa de la Mina go straight on, avoiding a right turn downhill. The twisty road is not surfaced and has no protection at the side, so take care. Continue for a further 6 km to reach the ruined inn of El Daire, and keep going. A further 4 km of bendy dirt road will bring you to a crossroads. Turn left.

A couple of kilometres further on you will reach a pass, where a track comes up from the right. This is Puerto Blanquillo. Just beyond it the track widens and is a good parking place.

- Walk on the track going east. You will soon reach a fork in the track. Keep right. You should see El Cisne, the mountain with two peaks, and with a prominent pine tree between the two. I guess it got its name The Swan because the peaks resemble wings. The track leads you downhill towards the source of the Río Higuerón. There is a reservoir here for firefighting. Do not go right down to the reservoir but stay on the dirt track above the water tank. It starts to ascend, and crosses a stream at a very sharp right turn. The track becomes concrete for a short distance. Go round a left-hand bend, and then look for cairns on the right indicating the start of the ascent to the peak, which towers above you.

- Turn right at the cairns. The route enters a gully, but almost immediately goes up to the right, out of the gully and ascends the hill on a path that has recently been much improved (2017). The route is now fairly easy to follow, but if in doubt keep near to the gully. At one point the cairns lead you back into the gully and out again on its left. There is then a very narrow and rocky stretch of path as it goes back into the gully. *There are cairns marking this point. Make a note of it, because you will need to remember it on the way back. It is easy to miss, and the gully below is impassable.*

- Ascend the gully for some way, and then follow the cairns over open ground once more. You will now be on the northern flanks of the mountain, with the peak high above on your right. Look up that way, and identify the gap between the two peaks. When you are more or less level with it look for a path ascending to the right. It can be difficult to spot, because the main path continues ahead and may seem more obvious. However, that is the return route. So, when about level with the gap above, look for some cairns going to the right, starting at about GPS ref. 421404 4078193.

- Turn right at this junction and follow the cairns. It is more of a route than a path, often crossing stony and loose ground. If in doubt aim straight for the col between the two peaks, where a lone pine tree stands. As you near the col the route is confusing, but cross to the left. The final ascent is via a narrow gully all the way over to the left-hand side of the broad valley you are ascending.

- Once you reach the tree it is an easy scramble to the east, straight up to the main peak. There is a short ridge with great views. From the summit walk along the ridge to the east and a path leads down to the col below. Return to the pine tree, and then you can ascend the westerly peak easily enough. There is no path, but follow the left edge of the ridge. Take care because there is a sheer drop to the left, but there is room to stay away from it if you wish.

- Return again to the pine tree. Then turn left (northeast) to take a path that circuits around the back of the second peak. You will descend straight away into a tricky gully, but once again cairns mark the way. This is the most difficult part of the walk, as it goes steeply down on loose and slippery ground. Keep well over to the left. The path improves as it leaves the gully and leads on to a minor col and goes to the left.

- Once out of the gully follow the cairns, which will take you all the way back to the junction where you left the main path on the ascent. Then return by the outward route. You should have no real difficulty following the path down, but when it returns into the gully *watch for the point mentioned above where I told you to make a note of it*. The path leaves the gully on the right-hand

THE PEAK OF EL CISNE

side over some rough stony ground. It would be easy to go too far. If you arrive in the gully at a precipice you have gone too far, so retrace your steps a little to find the path.

- Once you have passed this key point in the walk, just follow what remains of the path down to the dirt track and turn left to return to Puerto Blanquillo.

You must take care on this walk not to lose your way, and remember that if you have an accident nobody may pass by for months (literally).

APPROXIMATE GPS REFERENCES (UTM)

Start	419219 4077299
Beginning of path	420520 4078344
The gully	420666 4078251
Right turn	421404 4078193
Main summit	421596 4077879
Going down	421774 4078095

El Lucero south side – **WALK 16**

WALK NO. 23

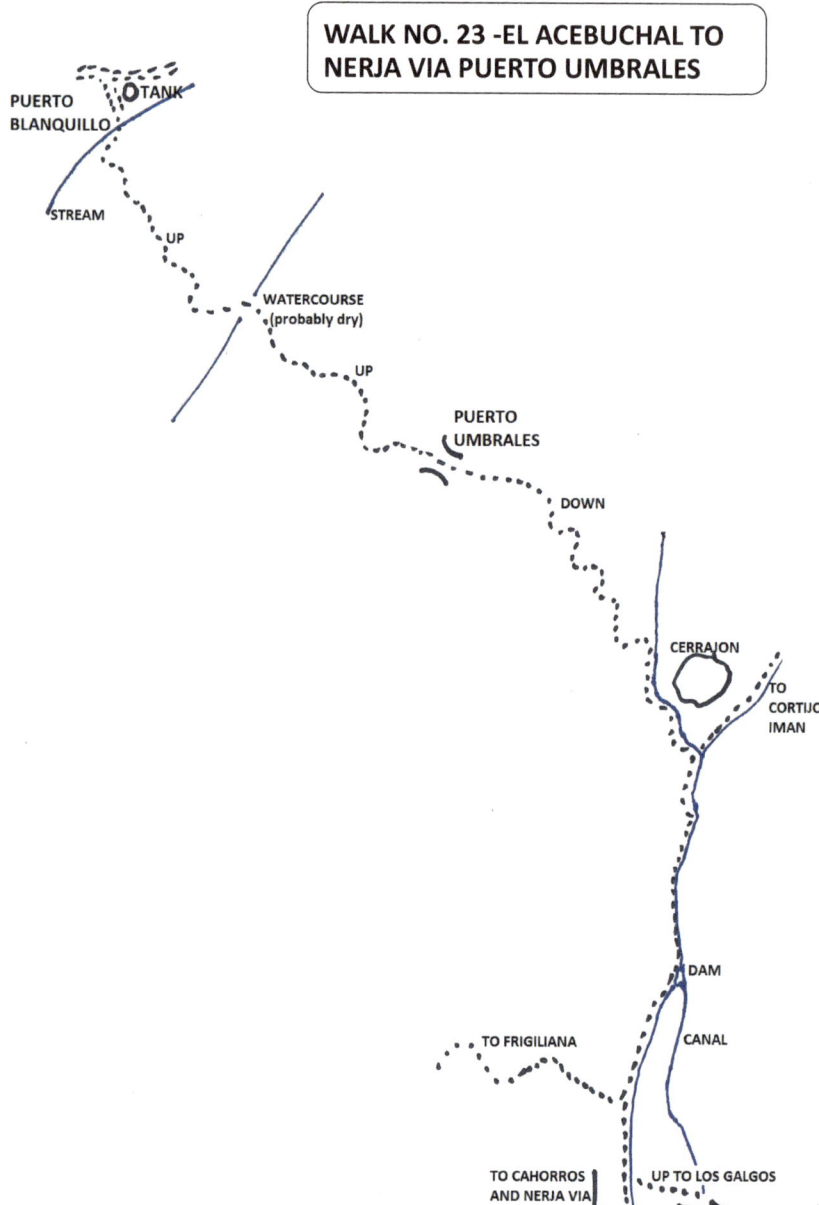

WALK NO. 23

EL ACEBUCHAL TO NERJA VIA PUERTO UMBRALES

A linear walk through high mountain passes and river valleys to the coast

Distance	18 km or 20 km linear
Ascent	850 metres or 1,200 metres
Overall grade	Strenuous
Terrain	Footpaths
Exposure	None
Highest point	1,033 metres

The walk begins at El Acebuchal. Since this is a linear walk it would be good to arrange transport at one end or the other.

You could shorten the walk by 4 kilometres, and reduce the total ascent by 350 metres, by starting at Puerto Blanquillo. However, to get there you would need a four-wheel drive. Puerto Blanquillo can be reached by dirt road from El Acebuchal via the old quarry above the village, or from Cómpeta via Casa de la Mina.

The sketch map covers the section between Puerto Blanquillo and the Río Chillar. For El Acebuchal to Puerto Blanquillo see Walk 20. At the end of the walk the optional route through Los Cahorros needs no map, and for the option via Los Galgos see Walk 25.

From the bars in El Acebuchal walk to the north-eastern end of the village. At the right-hand bend walk straight on into the valley, which is signposted (red and white bands on a post) as part of the long-distance route GR 242/GR 249. There is a path that at times leaves the valley bottom, but rejoins it each time. A steepish ascent to the left leads you to a dirt track, where you should turn right to join another, more important track near a signpost saying *Venta de Cebollera*.

The *venta* is a ruined inn, out of sight beyond the track. A path leads up to it, but our route for this walk turns left instead and goes up the dirt track going north. You will soon reach another ruin with another signpost, also saying *Venta de Cebollera*. Continue up the dirt track to reach a junction where you should take the right fork, which is signposted *Puerta Verde*. This track/stream valley/footpath leads gradually uphill, with no real difficulties, until it joins a major dirt track at Puerto Blanquillo.

Turn right on the track and walk towards the twin-peaked mountain of El Cisne. Then, at a junction, take the right fork in the track and go downhill. You will see a water tank below on the right. Leave the main track and descend to this reservoir. Go round the right-hand side of the reservoir, cross the stream, and find the start of a footpath.

- The path initially follows the left bank of the stream but quickly swings left and uphill. It ascends steeply at first and then more gradually, traversing the southern flanks of the mountain El Cisne. The path may be somewhat overgrown at times. Apart from some bends in the path there is no other complication going up here. Keep going, gradually ascending in a south-easterly direction. A little over 2 kilometres from the start of the path it swings to the right and then back to the left, and at about 3 km it reaches the top of a pass, the Puerto de Umbrales.

- Past the top of the pass the path passes round a rocky bluff and commences a series of bends as it descends steeply down into a stream valley. Follow the path on this long descent all the way to the riverbed. If there is water in the stream (the Arroyo Pradillos) it will be very welcome on a warm day.

- Once you are at the stream turn right and follow the stream downhill. There are cascades in the river that have to be avoided. So keep your eyes open for a series of short paths, marked by cairns, which lead uphill away from the stream – only to descend to the stream bed again once past the waterfalls. There is normally no need to actually walk in the water in this stretch, as the water level is low except after heavy rain. However, *you should keep a keen eye open at all times for the cairns, which will enable you to avoid the impossible descents that would meet you in the stream bed. Should you arrive at the top of a precipice, go back and look for the cairns.*

- Continue following the stream for something over a kilometre and you will pass a hill (El Cerrajón) beyond which the stream joins the Río Chillar. Keep going south along the river, and after a further kilometre you will arrive at a dam and a small reservoir (a header tank for the local irrigation system).

- Cross the stream to reach the dam, and look for a canal, which you can follow by walking on the concreted side. There are some serious drops to the right, but they are fenced, so you should not have a problem unless you have severe vertigo. If you do, the alternative is to continue on the right bank of the stream, although it is seriously overgrown at the time of writing, If you take the canal route, stay on it for almost 1 kilometre until it crosses a good footpath (the GR249) where you can turn left. But if you wish to avoid the canal, from the dam continue on the path on the right bank as best you can. You will reach a point where a path goes uphill to the right. This is the route to Frigiliana, but for this walk ignore it. Continue on the right bank of the river on part of the long-distance path GR 249, and very shortly you have another choice to make.

- *Choice 1* is to cross the river and then follow the GR 249 path uphill.
- You will soon reach the irrigation canal which comes from the dam. Stay on the path gradually uphill until it reaches a broad dirt track. Turn right along the track and you will reach the col of Los Galgos. You can then follow the ridge over Cerro Mangueno as in Walk 25, and continue down to Nerja.
- *Choice 2* is to stay on the right bank of the river. It is a shorter route, with less ascent, but you will soon have to walk into the riverbed. This is a terrific section, where the river goes through *Los Cahorros*, a narrow gorge. It should not be done after heavy rain, because you have to walk in the river itself. Even in normal conditions you will get wet to the knees or higher. The canyon is so narrow that you can touch the walls on each side. If you go this way, when you leave the Cahorros follow the broad, stony riverbed past an electric station and then into a disused quarry. From here a surfaced road will take you into Nerja after about a further kilometre.

APPROXIMATE GPS REFERENCES (UTM)

El Acebuchal start of path	417646 4075102
Venta Cebollera	418260 4075901
Path near stream	420180 4078202
Puerto Umbrales	421815 4076957
Stream	422835 4076121
Río Chillar	423139 4075361
The Dam	423132 4074694
Choice of routes	422838 4073943
Canal meets GR249 path	423027 4073816
Collado Los Galgos	423739 4073011
Quarry	421522 4069896

WALK NO. 24

FRIGILIANA TO THE SUMMIT OF EL FUERTE

A half-day walk from the village of Frigiliana to the summit of El Fuerte, the hill that dominates the northern side of the village.

Distance	9 km round trip
Ascent	730 metres
Overall grade	Easy
Terrain	Footpaths
Exposure	None
Highest point	1,007 metres

Although this is not a long walk any hill walker who visits Frigiliana will want to do it, and the views from the summit make it well worthwhile.

Starting in Frigiliana, make your way to the very topmost part of the village, with your compass set to take you due north. Above the town, beyond a concrete track that goes from south-east to north-west, there is a hill with the remains of an old castle, the Castillo de Lizar. Beyond it is a water tank, the Pozo de Lizar. Just beyond that a marked path leads you up to the north and away into the hills.

Once you are on the path all you have to do is follow it. It is a well-walked route and you should have no trouble finding your way. There are no practical alternatives.

The path ascends steadily, sometimes through pine trees and sometimes in the open. It goes along the crest of a broad ridge. As with all paths, tracks and roads in this area, the path twists and turns, but after about 0.5 of a kilometre from the start of the path the general direction swings from northerly to north-westerly.

WALK NO. 24

About 400 metres before the summit the path veers to the left (west), with the hilltop to the right. Follow it round, and then walk up to the right to reach the top. The summit marker is at 984 metres. Just along a short ridge there is a higher point at 1,007 metres, although there is no path to take you there.

The views from the summit are rewarding, with the coastline to the south, and virtually the whole of the Sierra Almijara inland.

From the top, simply reverse your steps to Frigiliana.

A sketch map for this walk is not really necessary.

APPROXIMATE GPS REFERENCES (UTM)

Frigiliana	420192 4072064
Path up	420044 4072513
Summit	418464 4074655

Venta Panaderos – **WALK 19**

WALK NO. 25
NERJA TO COLLADO LOS GALGOS VIA THE RÍO CHILLAR

This walk starts near the coast and contains a bit of everything: river valleys, broad ridges, remote landscapes and good views.

Distance	17 km
Ascent	950 metres
Overall grade	Moderate
Terrain	Footpaths
Exposure	None
Highest point	674 metres

From Nerja you need to find the disused quarry where the Río Chillar reaches the edge of town. A good, recently concreted track from near the end of Calle Picasso leads you below the motorway to the quarry and cement works. You can park by the cement works. At weekends it may be busy. If so, nearer town there is an overflow car park for people walking into the Cahorros of the Río Chillar.

- From the cement works walk into the river valley, passing immediately by the disused quarry. After only 0.7 kilometres take a vague and unmarked path up the hillside to the right. (Take care to find the right path. If you reach a building on the right with an electric turbine you have gone too far.) The path improves as you ascend. It leads quickly to a 'dingly dell', where old quarry workings have left a lovely green valley. From here a path goes down to the left but you should go upwards, keeping to the right. As you leave the dell you will be on a good footpath through the Barranco del Tranco. The path ascends.

- Continue up the path through pine forest. You will be travelling mainly east although the path takes a zigzag route, still ascending. You will then cross some open ground and the path veers to take a more southerly direction and then swings to the east again to lead you to the top of a ridge, where you will find a junction of paths. Turn left here to stay on the broad ridge, and now head north-east on Cerro Boniato. (If you turned right the path would lead you to Capistrano at the east end of Nerja.)

- The ridge leads you along to ascend Cerro Mangueno, at an altitude of 674 metres. After crossing the hill – and still following the same ridge – you will reach a junction with some cairns, where you should avoid a left turn and keep going slightly to the right (north-east). *Make a note of this point for later reference.* The ridge now leads you on to the col of Los Galgos, where you will meet a broad dirt track coming up from below on the right (where you can see the El Pinarillo picnic site in the valley bottom).

- Do not take the track down to the right, but instead take a track straight ahead. This track would eventually lead you to the dam in the higher reaches of the Río Chillar. But for this walk continue for just less than a kilometre and turn left downhill on a footpath, where the red and white paint indicates that you are on the GR 249 path.

- After 0.5 km on this path you will reach an irrigation canal, and the return route commences here. Turn left along the side of the canal. It is an exciting route, high above the valley of the Río Chillar below, and shortly you will reach a really spectacular section of path, which goes through and around a cliff face. It is fenced, so unless you have severe vertigo you should have no problems. However, stay on the path and do not take unnecessary risks.

- *Until recently the next part of this route followed the canal for 4 kilometres, with some fairly airy sections that were not suitable for anybody without a head for heights. However, a fence was recently erected along here. Very soon afterwards it came down again, but there is a sign saying that the route is closed, so I have amended the walk in order to avoid this section. If you do decide to continue along the canal take great care of the drop to the side. But you are advised to follow the route described below instead.*

- Approximately 1 kilometre from joining the canal a cairn marks the start of a path uphill to the left. Take this path, which, in a distance of less than half a kilometre and ascending steeply, will lead you back to the Collado Los Galgos. Turn right here and take the path along the ridge, retracing your steps on the outward route for a short distance.

- Stay as close as you can to the crest of the ridge, and after about 1.25 km you should find the cairns that you passed earlier, shortly after leaving Cerro Mangueno. This time take the right turn and follow the right-hand (south-westerly) ridge. About 1 km farther on the path swings to the right, and then begins a steeper descent towards the valley of the Río Chillar.

- You will soon reach the western end of the irrigation canal, having avoided the vertiginous section (and the fence). Continue on the path, which goes to the left and then takes some serious zigzags as it descends what is now a steep hillside. Continue downwards to pass below a wall and alongside a pipeline descending from the canal.

- As you near the bottom of the hill you will discover the reason for the pipeline. There is an electricity generating station there. You will probably hear the hum of the turbine. Keep to the left side of the valley as you descend and go down some steps to reach the river valley below.

- Once you are in the broad, stony valley of the Río Chillar, simply take a left turn and follow the stream back to the quarry near Nerja.

APPROXIMATE GPS REFERENCES (UTM)

Path to the right	421508 4070462
On the path	422626 4070242
Turn left	423031 4070426
Cerro Mangueno	423201 4071303
Junction	423031 4072113
Collado Los Galgos	423739 4073011
Path down	423526 4073603
Canal	423031 4073806
Path up	423353 4073083
Junction (again)	423031 4072113
Far end of canal	421703 4071626

Sierra Almijara from Puerto Collado – **WALK 11**

WALK NO. 26

WALK NO. 26 - MARO VIA EL PINARILLO TO FRIGILIANA OR NERJA

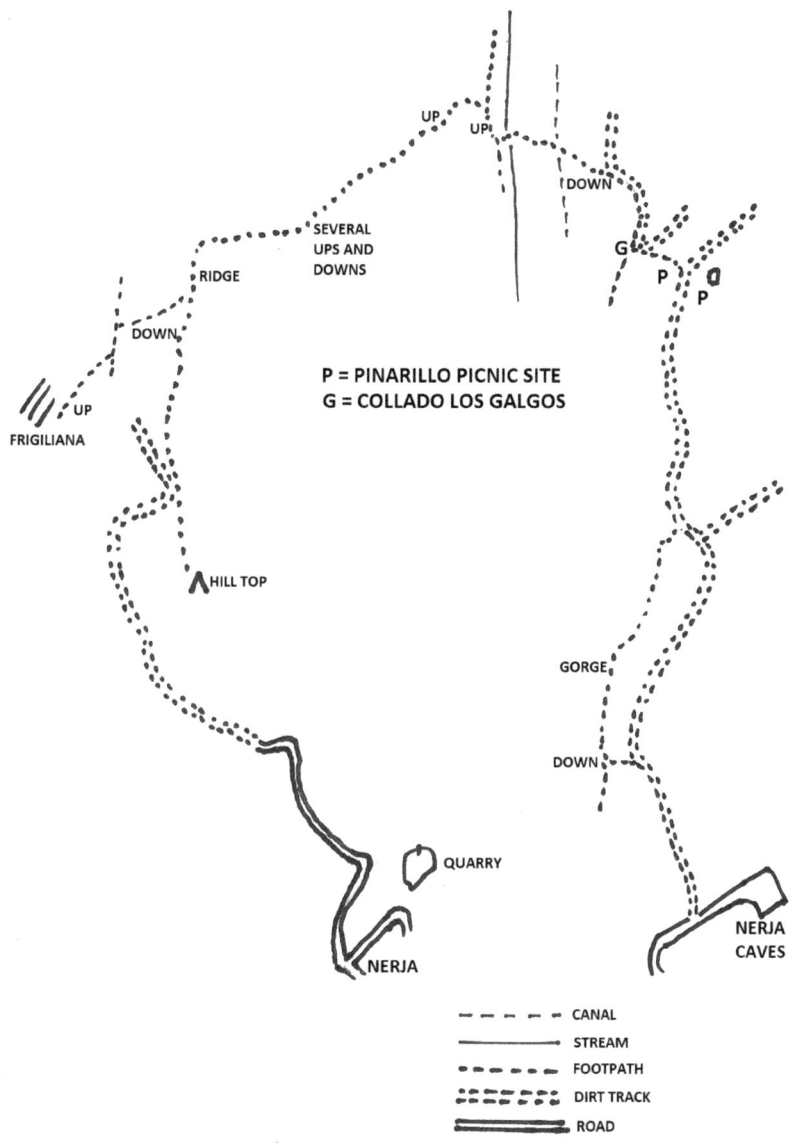

WALK NO. 26
MARO VIA EL PINARILLO TO FRIGILIANA OR NERJA

A walk from near the coast to the beautiful village of Frigiliana, via a high level route with a river crossing. There are repeated ascents and descents, and a river crossing that can be a bit tricky after heavy rain.

You have two options. One takes you to Frigiliana, making a walk of 15 kilometres with about 950 metres of ascent in total. The second option continues to Nerja, a walk of 18 km with almost 1,000 metres of ascent and descent – if you can, arrange for somebody to pick you up at the natural park boundary near the Río Chillar. Otherwise you will have some extra walking into town.

Distance	15 km or 18 km
Ascent	950 metres or 1,000 metres
Overall grade	Strenuous
Terrain	Footpaths
Exposure	None
Highest point	569 metres

On the N340, at a roundabout near Maro, follow the road signposted Cuevas de Nerja/Ladera del Águila. *Go past the Hotel Al Andalus on your left, and immediately before reaching the car park of the Cuevas de Nerja you will see a rough car park on the left. Park here and walk along a dirt road by a signpost saying* Parque Natural Sierras Tejeda, Almijara y Alhama.

This walk follows mainly what has now been designated as the GR 249. It is signposted with red and white marks intermittently along the walk. But my directions lead you along slightly different routes at times.

- From the car park follow the broad, main track past a traffic barrier, which is normally open. There is a gorge below to your left. Keep it there for the time being. After 1.3 kilometres on the track turn left on to a path marked by cairns. It leads you down over some rocks to the bottom of the shallow gorge. Turn right along the gorge, which has cliffs and caves to either side. Continue for 1.9 km, and then look out for a track leading up to the right. The bottom of this track has been washed away, but it is passable. Follow the track out of the gorge. (You will know if you go too far because you will reach the vertical wall of a dam.)

- The track now takes you uphill to reach the main dirt track that you left earlier. Follow it to the left. After walking for a quarter of an hour you will reach a concreted stretch of track, where you can take a footpath to the left to cut out some bends. Once you have joined the main track once more, follow it to the left to reach the picnic area of El Pinarillo, which is about 5 km into the walk and a good place for a rest.

- Turn left off the main track at El Pinarillo, walk to the far left side of the picnic site, and look for a track going down to the right past a metal barrier. It has a GR 242 sign to help you find it. Follow this into a valley and up the other side, taking a path going uphill to the left from the track. This soon reaches another, broader track, which you should follow to the left to reach a col, the Collado Los Galgos. You will now be looking down into the valley of the Río Chillar, with higher ground to your right and to your left. A path goes straight ahead down the other side of the col. But ignore this, and instead turn right along a track going north, on the western flanks of a hill (the Cerro del Águila).

- After a little less than a kilometre you will reach a marker post indicating the start of a path to the left going down into the valley. Take this path, cross an irrigation canal, and keep going down all the way until you reach the Río Chillar. Cross the river/stream as best you can. Often it is not a problem, but after heavy rain it can be difficult. When you reach the stream it is best to go 50 to 100 metres upstream, where the rocks there can make it easier to cross.

- On the far side take a path to the right that follows the river uphill. After a few minutes look for another path going up to the left. There is an arrow pointing to Frigiliana, and once more it is signposted as the GR 249 . Take this path and ascend in zigzags, and then descend on the other side of a ridge. Continue climbing and descending repeatedly until, 3.5 km from leaving the Río Chillar, you will arrive at the top of a ridge. Here you have a choice to make.

- The shorter option goes to the village of Frigiliana, from where you can take a bus or a taxi back to Nerja and Maro. The longer option takes you directly to Nerja on foot. (Personally I prefer the Frigiliana option, because it avoids a long walk through town.)

- For the Frigiliana option, on reaching the ridge cross the crest of the ridge, going to the west. A path descends steeply in zigzags to reach the Río Higuerón. At the bottom turn left alongside the river, cross over to pass a water tank, then continue on the far side of the river. Look for a path going uphill to the right, which will lead you into the village of Frigiliana.

- For the Nerja option, ignore the path descending from the ridge and continue on a less well-defined path that keeps to the very top of the ridge going south. It is rather a poor path at times, but marked with cairns, and if you keep to the ridge top you will not go far wrong. At one point on a small summit the ridge separates into two ridges. Keep to the one on the left and continue along the top, looking down into the lower reaches of the

Río Chillar below on your left. The path leads you to a clearing where a broader dirt track comes up from the right. Here another path goes straight on to ascend the hill ahead, but ignore it and go along the dirt track to the right instead.

- The track descends on a zigzag route. You can take a shortcut through some of the bends on a path to the left, then join the track again. It becomes a concrete track and starts to pass houses on the outskirts of Nerja. There are lots of options as you go along, but if you keep taking the left turn at all times you will eventually arrive at the Río Chillar, near a quarry and a cement works. If you have prearranged transport they can pick you up there. (To find it your driver needs to take Calle Picasso from Nerja, head for the Central de Electricidad of the Río Chillar, and park by the Parque Natural signpost.)

- If you do not have transport waiting you will need to walk into Nerja. To do so just follow the road. It is still a couple of kilometres into town. I walked back to my car at Maro, but that was 5 km from reaching the road near the cement works, so your own transport or the bus from Nerja may be better.

APPROXIMATE GPS REFERENCES (UTM)

Start	424381 4068793
Path to the left	423785 4069731
Pinarillo	424128 4072621
Collado Los Galgos	423739 4073011
River crossing	422837 4073962
Path left	422886 4074104
Ridge	422886 4074104
Frigiliana	420294 4072077
Keep right (Nerja route)	420847 4071368
Río Chillar	421522 4069896

FUENTE DEL ESPARTO TO THE PEAK OF NAVACHICA

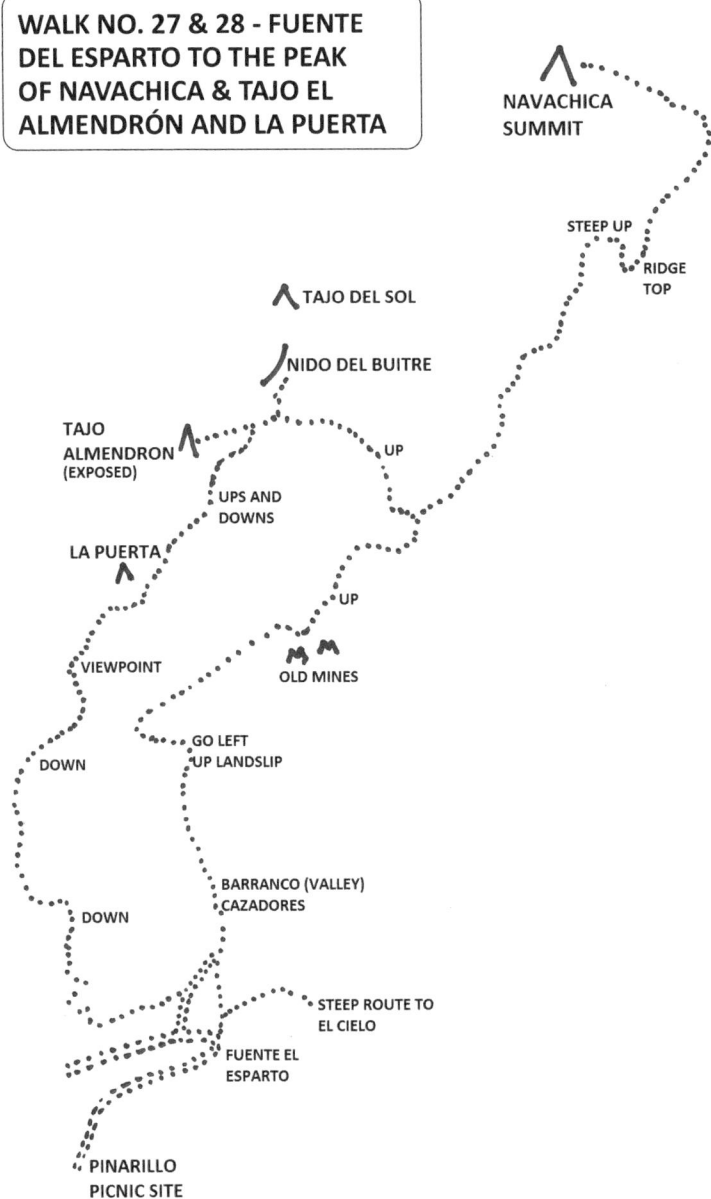

WALK NO. 27

FUENTE DEL ESPARTO TO THE PEAK OF NAVACHICA

A very strenuous full day's walk, ascending to the summit of Navachica (1,832 metres), the highest point in the Sierra Almijara.

Navachica is not an imposing peak. It is a rounded hilltop of bare rock and prickly undergrowth. But it is wild and remote, and because it is the highest in this sierra it is worth conquering. There is no easy way to get there (unless you have a helicopter).

Distance	17 km
Ascent	1,350 metres
Overall grade	Very strenuous
Terrain	Footpaths
Exposure	None
Highest point	1,832 metres

The route commences at a curve in the dirt road close to Fuente del Esparto, which is reached on foot or by car along a track that starts immediately opposite Las Cuevas de Nerja (the Caves of Nerja), which are near Maro. From the autovía *(the dual carriageway) take the roundabout where the Cuevas de Nerja are signposted, go past the Hotel Al Andalus. With the entrance to the* cuevas *on the right, turn left to cross a rough car park and pass through a barrier (normally open) to follow a broad track approximately 5 kilometres to the picnic site of El Pinarillo. On the way take the left fork at a junction. Continue past the picnic site for a further 1 km and park where the track takes a sharp turn to the left, at the foot of the Barranco de Cazadores (the Hunters' Valley).*

Ensure that you take plenty of water. This is a big ascent, and there is no water at all en route.

- From the apex of the bend, walk into the valley. You will pass some old cave dwellings. This was at one time the scene of major mining activity. Continue walking along the valley bottom and ignore two paths going off to the right which are marked with cairns. Also ignore a track going up to the left. Stay in the valley, walking on rough, stony ground, until after about twenty-five minutes' walk you will reach a point where a heavily eroded gully goes up to your left. There are cairns and red paint marks, which can be difficult to spot, but turn left up here and then keep well over to the right-hand side of the eroded area, from where a decent path ascends the hillside. This route avoids the precipice that blocks the valley bottom.

- So, ascend this path, and then turn right along an old mining path. This takes you above a high waterfall (normally dry) and then meets the valley floor again, before climbing once more to a point where you will pass a fenced mineshaft on the left side of the path. Then you will see mineshafts (the *Mina de Furia*) in the valley below on the right. Continue on the path to the left, above the mines.

The route is easy to find at this stage. It ascends gradually, keeping above the left side of the *Barranco de Cazadores*. After zigzagging up you will reach a small promontory with a view back down the *barranco*, but the path continues uphill to the right of the platform. After the valley bottom has come up to meet you once more you will find some cairns on the left side of the path marking the route up to the peaks of El Almendrón and Tajo del Sol (see Walk 28). Ignore this turn, and stay on the path straight ahead in the *barranco*.

A little further on you will reach the junction of two *barrancos* (valleys or gullies). Take the left fork into the Barranco del Rey, keeping to the trodden route. You will very soon pass a possible turn into another valley on the left, but ignore it. Keep going and follow the bed of the valley, scrambling over rocks as you go. This section is rough and tough. Some 200 metres farther on, look for cairns marking a steep and difficult path uphill to the right. It is very easy to lose the path, so take care. I In fact there are two ways up this hill, both of them tough going. The important thing is to follow the cairns and to reach the top of the ridge (at GPS 427076 4076509). You will now have views back towards El Almendrón, and, to the south-east, of the hills leading to El Cielo. Navachica is the summit of the open moorland to the north

- On reaching the ridge, follow it to the north-east. There is a path at times, and there are cairns to mark the way. Keep to the left below the first top and aim for a lone pine tree, from where you will ascend the hillside to the north to reach the top of a broad ridge. Here you should turn left for the summit of Navachica, probably some four and a half hours from the start of the walk.

- From the summit return by the outward route. Walk back along the first broad ridge and descend to the right. Watch carefully for the cairns because *it is very easy to stay on higher ground, which would lead you into the wrong valley*. You MUST find the cairns and follow them. Of course, if you are using GPS you can track back.

- At GPS 427076 4076509 there is a small outcrop. One of the two descent paths begins on the right just a couple of metres before it, and the other starts just beyond it. I would say that the second path gives an easier descent to the valley bottom and it avoids some of the difficulties in the valley bottom.

Once you are in the valley bottom, follow it all the way back to the start along the outward route

FUENTE DEL ESPARTO TO THE PEAK OF NAVACHICA

APPROXIMATE GPS REFERENCES (UTM)

Start	424899 4073197
Up to the left	425021 4074744
Viewpoint	425447 4075146
Mines	425620 4075355
Ignore path left	426031 4075458
Steep up to the right	426829 4076446
Alternative steep up	426920 4076612
Ridge	427084 4076516
High ridge (go left)	427696 4077389
Summit	427309 4077642

The south Lucero ridge – **WALK 21**

WALK NO. 28
TAJO EL ALMENDRÓN AND LA PUERTA

A walk up the huge Cazadores gully, to a col with a great view and an optional, exposed scramble to the peak of El Almendrón. The peak can be seen from the coast. It is distinguishable as a knife-edge limestone ridge.

Distance	15 km
Ascent	1,050 metres
Overall grade	Strenuous
Terrain	Footpaths
Exposure	None except near the peak, where there is a huge drop. But those who prefer to can avoid it
Highest point	1,515 metres

This walk begins near Fuente del Esparto, which you will find beyond the picnic area of El Pinarillo, 6 km along the dirt track that starts opposite the entrance to the Caves of Nerja at Maro. The track passes the picnic area, and about a kilometre farther on it takes a sharp bend to the left, among eucalyptus trees, at the foot of the Cazadores gully. Park here.

Enter the Barranco de Cazadores (as described in Walk 27 to Navachica) and follow the same instructions as in that walk. But here is a summary. Stick to the main valley bottom (ignore paths to the right and then ignore a track to the left) until you are in an area of the valley where some cairns mark the ascent of the path to the left across a rockfall. Go left to ascend the rockfall but keep to its right-hand edge, where a path commences. Continue to the right at a higher level on an old miners' path, and after some more ascent pass above some mineshafts. Then continue ascending until the path levels out and two cairns and some red paint mark the beginning of a path to the left, at approximately 1,050 metres altitude (GPS 3426031 4075458). This is where you should leave the Navachica route and head up towards El Almendrón.

- The path ascends gradually in zigzags. At about 1,330 metres altitude (at GPS 425603 4075890) you will see the col called the Nido del Buitre (the Vulture's Nest) ahead and to the right. Go north to reach the col, where the views are terrific. There is a huge drop on the far side so take care near the edge, which is very exposed. As you ascend towards the col the path takes various forks, and you will need to choose the best route on more than one occasion. But, whichever path you take, aim to reach a place below and to the left of the col, at approximately GPS 425528 4075994 (Point A). Continue to the north to reach the Nido del Buitre, and then return to Point A. A faint path will then lead you further uphill to the left (south-west) and occasional blobs of paint will reassure you.

To ascend the El Almendrón peak it is easy enough to scramble up the northern side of the peak to within about 100 metres of the top, but please take care near the edge of the ridge. However, to reach the very summit you will need to go round to the western side of the peak, where a sloping ledge leads you above a precipice. This is a *very exposed* – if not very technical – section. *If you ascend it remember that you will have to come down it again.* I do not recommend this unless you are an experienced mountaineer.

- Return from the summit to its base and then descend to the right. There are several minor paths, and it is impossible to describe an exact route. Take any route downhill to the south-west and it should lead you to a better path, which will take a route to the south. The peak should now be above on your right. The path enters a rocky section, which requires some easy scrambling to get across. It is well marked with cairns.

There are some considerable ups and downs to deal with on this section. Keep watching for cairns and/or red paint marks.

- As you pass beyond the peak you will begin to descend, and the magnificent limestone monolith of La Puerta should be visible ahead. Continue on the path, which will now be easier, to pass below and to the left of La Puerta. (There is a cairn on the summit, but I think it would only be reachable by a roped-up rock climb.) As you reach the far side of the peak of La Puerta, and just before the next hill starts, turn right and follow a path for a short distance to reach a col with a lone pine tree and another magnificent view down into the valley of the Río Chillar. Take care here, as it is a serious drop. You should see the ruined Cortijo del Iman in a green meadow 2,000 feet or more below. The hills across the valley include El Fuerte, El Cisne and El Lucero.

- Return to the main path from this viewpoint and continue south-west. Cross an open area at just below 1,300 metres, and then go down a series of zigzags to gradually descend. At a point where at first glance you may think you are heading for a precipice, the path swings right, and away from danger.

- Continue to descend now without any great difficulty to eventually reach the beginning of a broader dirt track. Another path starts on the far side of the track. Take this path down, and when you next reach a track turn left along it. At a T-junction turn right, and at the next one turn left to get back to the bend in the road near Fuente del Esparto.

APPROXIMATE GPS REFERENCES (UTM)

Start	424899 4073197
Up to the left	425021 4074744
Viewpoint	425447 4075146

TAJO EL ALMENDRÓN AND LA PUERTA

Mines	425620 4075355
Path to the left	426031 4075458
Junction of paths	425603 4075890
Nido del Buitre	425584 4076162
Summit	425128 4075846
Main path for return	425474 4075934
On the path	425040 4075525
Viewpoint	424649 4075199
Turn right	425004 4073363
Turn left	424688 4073289

Descending La Maroma – **WALK 3**

WALK NO. 29

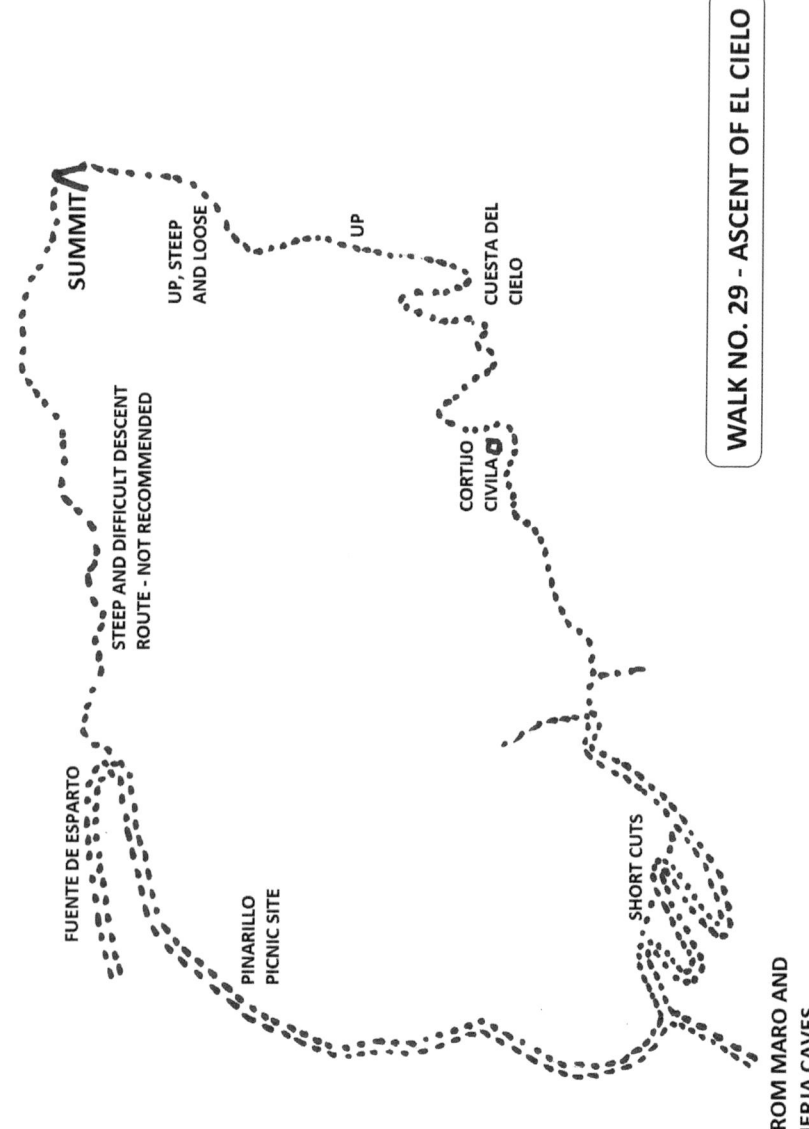

WALK NO. 29

ASCENT OF EL CIELO

An ascent of the peak which dominates the skyline from the coastal resort of Nerja. It rises to a height of 1,510 metres, but is only 6 kilometres from the Mediterranean coast.

Distance	14 km round trip
Ascent	1,250 metres
Overall grade	Strenuous
Terrain	Dirt tracks and footpaths
Exposure	None
Highest point	1,510 metres

On the N340, at a roundabout near Maro, follow the road signs to Cuevas de Nerja/Ladera del Águila. *Go past the Hotel Al Andalus on your left, and immediately before reaching the car park of the Cuevas de Nerja you will see a rough car park on the left. Drive across it and go along a dirt track, passing a barrier that is usually open. Continue on the track slowly (so you don't ground your car) for 3 kilometres and park near a junction of tracks.*

The sensible way to do this walk is as a linear route: out and back the same way. There is a circular route, but it is very difficult in terms both of steepness and of route-finding.

FOR THE LINEAR WALK:

- Leave your car at the fork in the tracks and walk up the right-hand track, which is signposted *Sendero del Cielo*. The track ascends continually, and in the early part of the ascent it takes some enormous zigzags. You can take a shortcut through at least the first two bends on footpaths, which are steeper but save distance.

- Continue on the track for about 3 kilometres (assuming that you have taken the shortcuts). About 1.5 km along you will pass a path going up to the left and then another going down to the right behind a building. Ignore these and stay on the main track until you reach the ruined buildings at Cortijo La Civila.
- The track circuits the buildings, and you can go round the front or the back as you wish. It continues as a broad track, now going north, and then shortly becomes a footpath. It goes into a long series of zigzags as it climbs the hill.
- Approximately 2.5 km from the cortijo you will reach the crest of a ridge with great views in all directions. The path swings left (north) and follows the top of the broad ridge. The next kilometre is relatively steady going along the gradual rise of the ridge. But then you will reach the final ascent, which is another matter.
- The path takes a route to the left (western) flank of the summit pyramid, and ascends steeply over bare, stony ground – which is also loose and slippery – to reach the summit, which is marked with a large cross as well as with a trig point.
- Alternatives from the summit are:

Return by the outward route. (The vast majority of walkers do so.)

Continue over high ground with no path all the way to the summit of Navachica. This is quite achievable but there is no path, so it requires good navigation and is a very big day.

Take a path from the summit of El Cielo down to the west and into the Barranco de la Higuera, and thence to Fuente del Esparto. This can be done, but it is difficult to find and is a very steep descent. I do not recommend it.

ASCENT OF EL CIELO

APPROXIMATE GPS REFERENCES (UTM)

Start	424279 4071114
Junction of paths	425386 4071600
Cortijo La Civila	426348 4072055
Summit	427283 4073527

View of Sierra Almijara

WALK NO. 30

WALK NO. 30 - THE PEAK OF LA LOPERA

WALK NO. 30

THE PEAK OF LA LOPERA

A short and easy walk on the eastern extremity of the Sierra Almijara Natural Park. It is in an area reached by a drive along a spectacular mountain road, and it is worth doing the drive even if you do not do the walk. It is a half-day walk, but you can combine it with a visit to a nearby restaurant, or a tour by car of the northern part of the sierras.

Distance	9 km
Ascent	320 metres
Overall grade	Easy
Terrain	Footpaths and tracks
Exposure	None
Highest point	1,487 metres

From the coastal village of Almuñécar take the road signposted to Otívar, passing underneath the main coastal road to go inland. You will pass through villages such as Jete and Otívar, and then the road climbs in zigzags to reach a height of about 1,300 metres. At one point the road is signposted Granada por la Sierra. *The views are spectacular. High in the hills you will pass an old building on the left of the road, the Mirador de la Cabra Monté, and several kilometres later you will see a signpost on the left saying* Sendero Pico Lopera. *Go on for a further half-kilometre to reach a restaurant on the left. The track to the left, alongside the restaurant, is also signposted* Sendero Pico Lopera. *Park here.*

- Walk along the track and then turn left through a gateway (a sign says it is open until 8.30 in the evening). You are now on the long-distance path GR 7, but that is incidental. Follow the track past the left side of the buildings of the Huerto Alegre Farm School . Continue on the track and ignore any minor turn-offs to the left. It swings right, passing some young walnut trees, and then left again to pass the Cortijo Prados farmhouse. There are some minor tracks, but keep to the main track, which gradually ascends until it meets another track coming from the right at the top of a slope.

- Turn left here. Go past a barrier across the track, which is for vehicles, and take the uphill (left) option at a junction just beyond the barrier. This track leads all the way to the top of La Lopera, where there is a trig point, and just beyond it a fire watch station and a signpost with faded letters. The view is splendid in all directions, with the Sierra Almijara peaks of Navachica and El Lucero to the west, the coast down below, and the Sierra Nevada to the east.

- Turn left at the fire watch station. Follow a stony route to the north-east along a firebreak to reach a path after about 250 metres. Turn right on the path, and 700 metres further down the hill there is a junction. Swing sharp left here (or you can take a shortcut if you wish at GPS 432336 4081398), and then after a little more than 100 metres go to the right again on a less well-defined path. Follow this through the woods, with several bends in the path, until it swings left on to a broader track, reaches a very nice clearing, and then joins the outward track once more. Turn right to return to Huerto Alegre and your car.

APPROXIMATE GPS REFERENCES (UTM)

Start	434306 4081519
Left turn	431565 4082423
Left fork	431584 4082162
Summit	431856 4081051